PHOTO BY LOW AND INSIDE

••• INSIDE YOU'LL FIND •••

OPEN APRIL-NOVEMBER
PLEASE CHECK OUR WEBSITE FOR
CURRENT HOURS OF OPERATION
**28995 LANSING ROAD
DYERSVILLE, IOWA 52040**
563.875.8404 DIRECT
888.875.8404 TOLL FREE
FIELDOFDREAMSMOVIESITE.COM

Welcome to my land. Many of you have come from distances to experience the majic or are interested in reading about me. I'm around for all of you to enjoy. Please respect my visiting hours from April through November (please check website for current hours of operation). This place is special to many people for many different reasons.

Admission is free and there is a souvenir stand with a wide variety of things to choose from. People find me interesting to visit. I encourage you to sit and dream on the bleachers, swing a bat or even toss around a baseball. Get together with other people who have gone the distance and become aquainted. I guess you could say that I'm one of those places you don't just look at but can experience for yourself in your own personal way. I only ask that you respect me and remember the next guy who hasn't gotten the chance to see me yet.

There have been thousands that have gone out of their way, not really sure what to expect or why they are driving to this small city in northeastern Iowa—but they continue to come from all over the world.

Some have called me a "little piece of heaven on earth." I am a Field where reality mixes with fantasy, and dreams can come true.

PHOTO BY STEPHEN GASSMAN PHOTOGRAPHY

This official souvenir program should help you answer some of the many questions you have about me and my history. Who knows, perhaps you too will want to see me first-hand, be it the first or the seventh time. Each visit is a new experience.

Efforts are taken not to over-commercialize me. Anyone can visit when they have the chance. Hope to see you soon, or again I should say! Thanks for going the distance and enjoy your reading...

ORIGINAL OWNER DON LANSING   PHOTO BY LOW AND INSIDE

PERSONAL PRIORITIES
**Some dream of women
or fast cars,**

**Others of Hollywood
and movie stars.**

**But I dream of a ball field
that's graced with corn.**

**The kind of field
where memories are born.**

By Scott Mahlmann, Low and Inside LLC

CREDITS:
The **Field of Dreams Official Souvenir Program** was created in 1999. Historical information and content was updated for the **Field of Dreams 30th Anniversary** by **Low and Inside, LLC** in 2022.
Soft Cover ISBN#   978-0967379012
Hard Cover ISBN#   978-0967379029

Copyright ©2022 by **Low and Inside, LLC.** All rights reserved. Permission for any use of information within this publication request by email at creative@lowandinside.com. Graphic design and digital prepress by **Low and Inside, LLC;** Nick Vetter—President; Scott Mahlmann—Creative Art & Writing; Rads—The Get Down Get Funky Baseball Junkie. Email: creative@lowandinside.com **Photos for Purchase:** FieldofDreamsPhotos.com

Printed in the USA. A variety of sources were used to compile this publication. Referral to historical information relayed is covered under the Fair Use Doctrine of the United States Copyright Statute. The information contained could not have been done without the cooperation of many including: Don & Becky Lansing, Betty Boeckenstedt, Sue Reidel, Denise Stillman, Veda Ponikvar, Joe Thompson, Joe Scherrman, Dwier Brown, Keith Rahe, Mike Kalibabky, Joe Anders, Dan Wallach, Jacque Rahe, Roman Weinberg. A special thanks to Wendol Jarvis of "The Iowa Film Office" for all the time and materials from archives. The "Field of Dreams" ® trademark is owned by Universal City Studios, Inc. **PHOTO CREDITS:** Front cover by Stephen Gassman Photography; Back cover background and inset by Low and Inside; sky/corn page layout background by Low and Inside, LLC; All other photos contain photographer credit.

LOW AND INSIDE
LOWANDINSIDE.COM

The Field

Where boyhood dreams are fulfilled.
John M. French III; Sewickley, PA

A historical happening.
Charles & Betty Dego; Mesa, AZ

We saw the movie in Maryland and Guam—it's great, stirring message. Your Field makes it come to life for us. Thanks for keeping it here.
Bill & Rhonda Pypes; Coralville, IA

Our 30th anniversary trip to this area to see the Field was worth it!
Donald & Adrienne Savage; Mettawa, IL

Thanks W.P. Kinsella!
Amy McElroy; Park City, IL

Thank you so much today. I'd love to be back here some day in the future.
Yumi Aoki; Tokyo, Japan

Thank you for this shrine in Iowa.
Laird Coats; Verona, NJ

PHOTO BY LOW AND INSIDE

I melted...
Stan Smith; Elk, WA

Drove 900 miles...
Raymond Elias; Toronto, Canada

Keep it for our grandchildren.
Gordon & Lucille Richards; Waterloo, IA

I came all the way from Japan to see the Dream!
Lisa Heckman; Seattle, WA

Thanks for providing this emotional moment.
Joe Oegan; Des Moines, IA

Where fantasy meets reality!
Allan & Marge Planek; Naperville, IL

Came 200 miles out of our way for this. Thanks, we had fun!
Gary & Joan Campell; Denver, CO

PHOTO BY AMERICAN IMAGES

At 16 months my daughter is too young to realize what a great thing dreams are—but we're here and I'll tell her someday.
Nathyn & Kathleen Ballard; Houston, TX

We came too, Ray; my future in-laws have been trying to get me out here for two years now—it took the Field to get me to Iowa!
Pat Donohue; Packanack Lake, NY

I'm making a "home-run" today—Iowa my home state. Hats off to the best state in the Land.
Wayne Jackson; Earlville, IA

Thanks for leaving this Field here!
Janet Meneke; Conroe, TX

It's perfect...so perfect we came twice today and will return. Hope you can keep it going. It's like a mecca for baseball fans.
Richard & Elaine Cortews; Cumberland, RI

Hey, if I build one in Brooklyn...will the old Dodgers come back?
Laurie Giardeno; Brooklyn, NY

Thanks for keeping it alive!
Oooh, what a feeling!
Michael Buben & Buben Family; Buckey, AZ

Had a great time in the corn!
K.C. Family; South Bend, IN

This is great. Our grandson loved it!
Mick Michael Family; Lexington, KY

We came. We saw and we hit a ball!
The Termonts; Brasschaat, Belgium

PHOTO BY STEPHEN GASSMAN PHOTOGRAPHY

It's the first time I've dreamed with my eyes open!
Ashley Booth; Glenwood City, WI

It could be... It might be... IT IS!
Jacob Coons; Marysville, IN

The Field of Dreams is a state of mind.
Betsy Witt; Bemidji, MN

It was a long trip—but we came!
Fredric Nisson; Malmo, Sweden

FIELDSPEAK

**I've been called a little piece of heaven,
I've been claimed to be a magical place.
Where dreams have been conceived,
And memories have been embraced...**

PHOTO BY STEPHEN GASSMAN PHOTOGRAPHY

THE BEGINNING

"My father's name was John Kinsella. It's an Irish name. He was born in North Dakota, in 1896...and never saw the big city until he came back from France in 1918. He settled in Chicago, where he quickly learned to live and die with the White Sox. Died a little when they lost the 1919 World Series... died a lot the following summer when eight members of the team were accused of throwing that Series.

He played in the minors for a year or two, but nothing ever came of it. Moved to Brooklyn in '35, married Mom in '38, and was already an old man working at the Naval Yards when I was born in 1950.

things to fight about. We did. And when it came time to go to college, I picked the farthest one from home I could find. This of course drove him right up the wall, which I suppose was the point. Officially my major was English, but really it was the Sixties.

I marched, I smoked some grass, I tried to like sitar music...and I met Annie. The only thing we had in common was that she came from Iowa and I had once heard of Iowa. We moved in together. After graduation, we moved to the Midwest, and stayed with her family as long as we could. Almost a full afternoon.

We rented an apartment and I took a job selling insurance. I also drove a cab and worked in a pizza parlor. Dad died in June of '74. Annie and I got married that fall. A few years later Karin was born. She smelled weird, but we loved her anyway. Then Annie got the crazy idea that she could talk me into buying a farm.

I'm thirty-eight years old, I love my family, I love baseball, and I'm about to become a farmer. But until I heard "The Voice"...I'd never done a crazy thing in my whole life."

ABOVE PORTION FROM PHIL ALDEN ROBINSON SCREENPLAY FOR "FIELD OF DREAMS"

THE FIELD SPEAKS

All my life I have thought myself to be different from most; sometimes even special. Four generations of the Lansing family have lived happily in my house.

Over the years four more children were born. With the addition of Lucille, Irene, Viola and LaVerne, the house came alive with the laughter and tears necessary to raise a family while making a living off the land.

PHOTO BY LOW AND INSIDE

Catherine died of the flu in 1918 at the age of 35, with her youngest child LaVerne being just two-and-a-half years young. Joseph now faced raising five children alone. Catherine's sister would step in and assist in providing the family with the care that Catherine could no longer provide.

PHOTO BY WENDOL JARVIS

THE LANSING FARM AS IT ONCE LOOKED BEFORE STARDOM

My name's Ray Kinsella. Mom died when I was three, and I suppose Dad did the best he could. Instead of Mother Goose, I was put to bed at night to stories of Babe Ruth, Lou Gehrig...and the great Shoeless Joe Jackson. Dad was a Yankees fan then, so of course I rooted for Brooklyn. But in '58 the Dodgers moved away, so we had to find other

The Lansing Family Farm has been a part of the landscape since 1906. The land was purchased by Joseph and Catherine Lansing from widower Frank Meis on April 1, 1906. With their two-year old son, Lawrence, and another one on the way, they now called this farmstead home.

Years later, daughter Viola would recount her most treasured memories of this farm. "I remember growing up on the farm, which is now home to the 'Field of Dreams.' Our home was a warm, cozy place to be on a cold wintry night. Many were the times after chores were finished on the long winter nights, Dad would sit down and play cards with us

The main road leading up to me is called Lansing Road and has carried many harvested crops throughout the years, including corn, beans, oats

LANSING FAMILY: MOM (BERNICE), DON, MARY, BETTY, CAROL   PHOTO BY DON LANSING

AUTHOR W.P. KINSELLA   PHOTO BY LOW AND INSIDE

kids. There wasn't any television in those days, but we did have a radio or we would play a tune on the piano. Some nights my sisters and I would do embroidery work to pass the time," Viola concluded.

PHIL ALDEN ROBINSON   PHOTO BY MELINDA SUE GORDON

As adults, Lucille, Irene and Viola married and moved off the farm. Joseph sold some acreage to oldest son Lawrence, leaving LaVerne and his father the caretakers of the family homestead.

LaVerne married Bernice Kramer in 1939 and rented the farmstead from Joseph allowing him to continue to live with them. Upon Joseph's death in 1942, LaVerne and Bernice purchased the farm. In continuing the family legacy, Laverne and Bernice raised a family of four, MaryLou, Betty, Don, and Carol.

Time flew by until Don purchased the farm from his parents on May 20, 1979 and lived on the same land for many years.

and hay. There is a small stream running through the lowest portion of my confines that has been a source of water for livestock and a few crops for as long as I can remember. Nature has run its course here for years, let me tell you. It has been rather pleasant for me here!

It wasn't until the spring of 1988 that my true talent was discovered. Hollywood happened upon me and turned my life into what it is today! Talk about a fairytale story!

I guess you could say it all got started when a screenplay was written by Director/Screenwriter, Phil Alden Robinson in 1983. It was based on the book "Shoeless Joe" written by W.P. Kinsella who is a University of Iowa Writers Workshop Grad and now makes his home in Canada. Kinsella has written a number of baseball books during the years, some of which tie back to his Iowa roots.

The screenplay had been picked up by 20th Century Fox, but after four years abandoned the project. Universal Studios picked up the tab and put the screenplay into the works full force. That's

when Wendol Jarvis, who is the Manager of the Iowa Film Office, received the script. Wendol told me the story about how he started reading the thing around 10:30pm and, becoming teary-eyed with emotion, just couldn't put it down until it was completely read. Scripts are often sent to State Film Offices for review in the hopes of landing the right locations to film.

Iowa historically has not been thought of as the hot spot in America for movie-making, but you would be surprised at the titles with ties to Iowa settings. They include titles such as "Starman," "Bridges of Madison County," "Twister," "F.I.S.T.," "Michael," "Miles from Home," "Children of the Corn," and "Take This Job & Shove It," among many other productions.

Hollywood had been seriously considering filming their new movie in 20 other states before narrowing their selection down to Iowa, Illinois, and somewhere just outside of Toronto, Canada.

20TH CENTURY FOX ABANDONED THE SCREENPLAY AFTER 4 YEARS.

But just like most things in life, relationships can play a very important role. The "big shooters" from Hollywood were already familiar with some of my other buds in the area, so Wendol was fishing for new photographs of additional candidates for studio approval. As Manager of the Iowa Film

PHOTO BY WENDOL JARVIS   LANSING FARMHOUSE DURING THE SPRING OF 1988

WITH THE IOWA-FACTOR NOW IN PLACE, THIS IS WHERE I CAME INTO THE PICTURE!

Office, he received input from his area offices as well as various Chambers of Commerce. Suitable locations for projects are carefully selected according to predetermined criteria. These sites are then generally inspected by the studio in person for final approval. And, that's just what happened to me, too.

The next series of events helped determine my future forever. Universal Studios had decided to visit a number of farms one day in March of 1988, and Wendol had things all lined up for a visit to each site. Arriving in Dubuque, Wendol met up with Brian Frankish (Executive Producer) and Phil Alden Robinson (Director). They decided to grab a bite to eat at Mario's restaurant, which is located down-town. While inside Mario's, after about 45 minutes, Brian realized he had forgotten something out in the car and naturally went to get it. As he approached the car, his eyes got a bit bigger as he saw the trunk wide open! His heart rate increased as he ran over, expecting all his stuff to be missing, but he found everything in its place and quickly returned to Mario's to tell the guys about what had just happened. He said it was a far cry from California! This was a big deal as it demonstrated a valuable lesson for Hollywood on trust and the state of Iowa.

PHOTO BY WENDOL JARVIS   PHIL'S CREATIVE THOUGHT IN PROGRESS

The next lesson for the day occurred only a few minutes later. On the way to the restaurant, Wendol had offered to pay for their meals if Brian and Phil would pay the parking tab. Upon exiting the lot, the attendant requested a total of ten cents. This just blew the two producers away. They grabbed a receipt for the expenditure and sent it FedEx to Los Angeles, California (which probably cost around $11.00 to send). The movie project definitely could be done for less money in Iowa than by the favorite Canada, but Hollywood was still not 100% convinced to set up in the Dubuque area.

PHOTO BY WENDOL JARVIS   PHIL ALDEN ROBINSON PLAYING OUT A FEW SCENES

One other element fell into place that sealed the deal. In 1988 a new Interstate (I-20) was being constructed across Iowa. In Dubuque, a building slated for demolition was sold to Universal Studios for $1. This building could be used to house their offices during the filming process. Comparing costs, Canada could not compete and Iowa won the bid!

With the Iowa-factor now in place, this is where I came into the picture! Hundreds of rolls of film had been shot, depicting farms around Iowa, by several respective film reps. These were then forwarded to Hollywood. Sue Reidel, who is a member of both the Dubuque and Iowa Volunteer Film Boards, was the first person to spot me along with my potential! Her criteria to meet as described by Universal Studios was a traditional, all-American farm; a house two-stories high, white in color and set apart by itself with a long driveway, and resembling a one-man operation with a barn and all the other identities that pop into your mind when you say the word "farm." Another important requirement was that the farm had to be surrounded by cornfields and set within some soft, gently-rolling hills for location lighting and to promote a sense of overall coziness.

At this point my ego was quite high, as I felt qualified after meeting all the criteria. I was just waiting for the right moment to come along. Sue travelled down many of the area's dusty, twisting roads looking for someone just like me. Sue stopped at many places to knock on doors and ask permission by the owners to take a photo of the properties she wanted to submit to Hollywood. When she first showed up to have a look at me, my owner, Don Lansing was not home. Sue liked the way I looked and so took my picture and submitted me anyway, along with the group of other places she had visited during that day. This still did not

assure me of my part in the play, but I had a good feeling about it all.

After Universal Studios narrowed the options down to a handful, the day arrived that I will never forget. I remember it was pretty cold, nearing February of 1988, I believe, when a car came rolling down Lansing Road. Inside were Wendol Jarvis, Phil Robinson, Brian Frankish, Dennis Gassner and Peter Harold, who were out scouting potential farms. I happened to be on the list of ones to see. All of the sudden, I heard this loud voice screaming, "Stop the car!" It was the voice of Phil Alden Robinson. The next sentence I heard from Phil was, "That's where I want to make my movie!" By this time I was feeling a little self conscious about all this commotion.

PHOTO BY WENDOL JARVIS   BRIAN FRANKISH & PHIL ALDEN ROBINSON

The car carrying these five guys came to a very quick stop along Lansing Road, just a few yards from me and I saw Phil jump out of the car, climb over the fence and run towards my house. I then saw the moment I will never forget—an artist envisioning his work. Phil was definitely in his role as he was swinging an imaginary bat and playing ball, picturing his well rehearsed script in his head. Things were finally clicking into place.

As the invisible bat was momentarily laid aside, Phil was already envisioning what it would take to make this dream happen. While calculating costs on paper, he began to list changes needed to keep

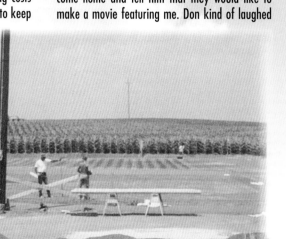

PHOTO BY WENDOL JARVIS   **WOODEN BLEACHERS BEING BUILT**

his screenplay true to form. I heard him say, "I want to add a white picket fence around by the house and the house will need a wrap around porch with a hanging swing right there. There's also a part in my movie where Ray Kinsella looks out his bedroom window. I think I'd like to add some bay

PHOTO BY DON LANSING   **LIGHTS BEING INSTALLED**

windows to the house for that scene. Also, let's re-rock the driveway, I want it to look very inviting. A few of those trees will have to go so I will have a spot for some lighting. What is that thing over there [pointing to my grain bin], I don't need that in my movie, so let's take it down. I might be from New York, but I once heard about how farmers tile the land. I think I would like to do that. Speaking of land, where should I build my field!" By now I was sweating a bit, wondering how I'd look if all this stuff were truly going to happen!

Both Peter Harold and Brian Frankish suggested that the logical place for the ballfield would be next to the lane coming into the farm. Phil however, felt strongly that I should be just where I am today. At that time a fence cut across my field dividing Don Lansing's farm from his neighbor. Universal Studios

would have to negotiate a separate contract to get me built correctly.

These five guys had been playing on my grounds for a few hours, and my owner, Don Lansing had no idea that they were here. They waited for him to come home and tell him that they would like to make a movie featuring me. Don kind of laughed and thought that they were just plain crazy. When the fact of where the sunset would fall was revealed by Don Lansing, Phil knew he had found his farm. Don then invited them all into my house where they discussed ideas and Phil made some more proposed adjustments to the interior of my house as he explained the gameplan. After negotiations and all that fine-print stuff, the deal was inked.

I had finally been discovered and was ready for my facelift. The first part consisted of all the things Phil had described originally. The second was building a regulation ballfield. The wrap-around porch outside the house was added to accommodate the porch swing. Bay windows were added to the end of my place to overlook the Field that would soon be built. The inside of my house was also remodeled to give it an open, airy feeling, and to make it easier for

THE REGULATION BALLFIELD BEING CONSTRUCTED

the cameras and crew while filming. By April of 1988, just before corn-planting was to begin, the crew was busy outside. My grain bin was taken down, the driveway was given a fresh layer of rock along with all the other little things Phil had requested. Then before I knew it, four of my

THE WHOLE BALLFIELD WAS CONSTRUCTED IN JUST FOUR DAYS!

evergreen trees were taken down and 28 truck-loads of dirt were brought in. My ground was leveled and marked off with stakes to strict regulation ballfield dimensions.

Nature played a trick on all of us during the summer of 1988. Before this growing season, I had not been so thirsty since the Dust Bowl days in the 1930s, it was very important that the corn be shoulder-height by the end of June, which is a rare sight in Iowa. With the assistance of several Iowa State agencies, the creek that runs through my farm was damned to form a reservoir. Water was piped from this to help quench my thirst a bit, but Iowa was in serious drought condition and the corn growth was behind schedule.

As the end of June neared, I was getting very anxious, but the corn had done so well, thanks to the irrigation measures, that is was too tall!

PHOTO BY WENDOL JARVIS   **NEW PENS BEING BUILT**

When Kevin Costner (Ray Kinsella) walked through the corn rows at the beginning of the film, he appeared too short! A wooden platform about a foot high was constructed for him to walk on as the camera rolled.

Now it was time to carve me out to my present day personality! The tractor used by Ray in the movie to plow under the corn belongs to my owner Don. It's a John Deere model 2640.

The whole ballfield was constructed in just four days. It happened during the Fourth of July weekend of 1988, as I recall. Everyone pitched in, including a few high school baseball teams from the Dyersville area. They showed up one day and laid seven semi-loads of sod on my field with care. My lighting was put into place overnight (which still works today), along with construction of my backstop and bleachers. I was now destined for stardom before millions of people!

Everything was just about perfect and my little piece of heaven on earth was looking like something right out of the movies! My facelift had left me wrinkle-free. My final accessory was the white picket fence. By this time I was getting really excited.

I was happy to see how all the ideas had come together. Now I was curious to hear who else would be cast to play in the movie with me. Besides Kevin Costner as Ray Kinsella, the cast included Amy Madigan as Annie Kinsella, James Earl Jones as Terence Mann, Burt Lancaster as Moonlight Graham, Gaby Hoffman as Karin Kinsella, Dwier Brown as John Kinsella and Timothy Bussfield as Mark—Annie's brother. This is just to name a few of the wonderful people who helped realize the dream that could happen.

PHOTO BY WENDOL JARVIS   **FARMHOUSE PAINTING**

I WAS NOW DESTINED FOR STARDOM BEFORE MILLIONS OF PEOPLE!

Originally, Jimmy Stewart had been cast to play the legendary Moonlight Graham. Mr. Stewart, who had a wonderful life, had become ill and was unable to play the part. The clip where Karin Kinsella is watching the movie "Harvey" (movie about an imaginary rabbit that would talk with Mr. Stewart and follow him around) while eating breakfast is a tribute to the late actor.

The subject of who would play Ray Kinsella was another interesting fandango, if you will. Universal Studios would have liked to have cast one of their

big cash contract actors to play as the main character and were leaning pretty heavily towards Jeff Bridges! Other candidates were Robin Williams, Steve Guttenburg, and finally my favorite, Jack Nicholson.

Kevin Costner was a relatively unknown actor when Phil Robinson first mentioned his name to me. He also told me Costner had a Gary Cooper-like way about him and thought he would work out just perfectly for the role of Ray. At this point, Costner had only landed a few roles on the silver screen including "Fandango" and "Silverado" along with just finishing up on "Bull Durham" which had not been released yet. With the success of "Bull

PHOTO BY DON LANSING   **LIGHTS INSTALLED**

PHOTO BY DON LANSING   **CORN IRRIGATION FOR FILMING**

Durham," Universal Studios increased the filming schedule for "Field of Dreams" from seven weeks to nine to help ensure the film's perfection. Additional scenes were then added to the shooting schedule.

One question I am frequently asked is what it was like hanging around with Kevin Costner he was a true gentleman. I must say it was a real treat seeing this actor bloom from the early years.

There is a cast member who I think, never gets enough credit for his acting role in the film. I think Dwier Brown (a.k.a. John Kinsella) actually played one of the biggest parts in the movie. I become

PHOTO BY WENDOL JARVIS   **INSIDE OF FARMHOUSE AS IT IS RECONFIGURED FOR FILMING**

7

nostalgic just thinking back to the scene when John and Ray Kinsella look at each other for the first time, especially the subliminal wording and portrayal of gestures relating father and son. Yes, their words were few, but they were strong. Personally, this is how Dwier's mannerisms actually are. He's a an honest man of few words who is a true professional actor.

with a sort of smile on his face. James Earl went on to explain to me how difficult it is to keep his voice intact and maintain the range. He mentioned that he prays everyday that he won't lose it at some point. His concern made me realize that what appears easy may be much more involved that you could ever imagine.

During a scene where Ray Kinsella was pitching to Shoeless Joe Jackson, Costner had to hit the dirt when Liotta almost hit him with a line drive. Instantly the director, Phil Robinson called for everyone to hold perfectly still. The great director

PHOTO BY DON LANSING   JAMES EARL JONES AND DON LANSING

FARMHOUSE KITCHEN COMPLETE WITH PROPS

PHOTO BY WENDOL JARVIS

PHOTO BY MELINDA SUE GORDON   PHIL ROBINSON IN ACTION

In the movie, Terence Mann was portrayed as being a reclusive writer. J.D. Salinger is the real-life wordsmith who ironically was born in 1919. Hollywood could not convince the writer to let them use his name in the film. They came up with Terence Mann who was brilliantly portrayed by James Earl Jones. When W.P. Kinsella wrote the book "Shoeless Joe," he used J.D. Salinger's name and later found out J.D. wasn't exactly happy to be included without permission.

Speaking of James Earl Jones, he was one of the nicest guys that you could ever meet. I can remember calling him "The Voice" one day (no, he is not my verbal identity) and he turned to look at me

PHOTO BY MELINDA SUE GORDON   LIVE FILMING FROM CORNFIELD

PHOTO BY DON LANSING   FILMING ON BALLFIELD

was in total control as he walked around and thought for a bit. He looked over at Costner and told him to stand up, dust yourself off and say to Shoeless Joe, "See if you can hit my curve-ball." This comment was then edited to be right before the line drive knocks him off his feet. It goes to show you that you cannot plan everything!

PHOTO BY WENDOL JARVIS

KARIN'S BLEACHER FALL SHOOTING

CREW IN ACTION FILMING WITH "ARCHIE GRAHAM"

FENWAY PARK IN BOSTON

Thinking fast, he directed Liotta to walk into the cornfield while the camera rolled. Within five-minutes the fog was so thick that all shooting had to be stopped. Fortunately they had achieved their goal. This out-take was later edited to occur after Ray and Shoeless had their first batting practice. It was further enhanced by George Lucas' Industrial Light & Magic Company to make it appear that Shoeless Joe literally disappeared as he walked into the corn.

propped everything into place including the signage and chickens in the windows detailing a Jewish area of Boston. During the filming of these scenes, some of the people of Dubuque were not quite sure what to think and called the Chamber of Commerce asking if a full-blown cultural invasion was going on. The only other location shot was at Boston's famous landmark, Fenway Park, home of the legendary Green Monster.

PREP WORK FOR THE BOSTON SCENE IN GALENA, IL

JAMES EARL JONES & HIS STAND IN

Another example of creative cinematography occurred during the scene when Ray Kinsella looked out the screen door and saw Shoeless Joe for the first time. While shooting, Robinson noticed fog was just beginning to roll in from the cornfield.

Most of the entire movie was shot on the Lansing farm in Dyersville, Iowa. There were a few location shots during the Moonlight Graham scenes done in nearby Galena, Illinois. The Boston street scene was devised in downtown Dubuque, Iowa. Hollywood

The scene depicting the apartment of Terence Mann in Boston was set inside the warehouse building Universal Studios bought for a dollar. The Boston skyline which appears through the window was actually a custom mural painting. (PHOTO ON PG. 15)

A relatively quick scene in the movie, familiar to all, is when Karin (Gaby Hoffmann) fell off the top of the bleachers and the legendary Doc Graham (Burt Lancaster) crossed over to revive her. The final cut was the result of many takes on a 90 plus degree Iowa afternoon. All angles were scrutinized over and over resulting in just the right look. Karin also had a case of the giggles during the filming of this scene, when Doc Graham would sort of tickle her as he came to her rescue. The end result is another perfect Hollywood clip.

BY THE MIDDLE OF AUGUST, 1988 IT WAS ALL OVER FOR ME— OR SO I THOUGHT.

PHOTO BY MELINDA SUE GORDON

JAMES EARL JONES AND KEVIN COSTNER

The movie's final scene required 1,500 cars driven by volunteers who answered an ad in the local newspaper offering free tickets to join the convoy. They all were treated to a picnic at Dyersville Commercial Club Park before the final scene was to be filmed. Every car was tuned to the local radio station which gave directions to the drivers of each car. The scene, orchestrated by helicopter, was shot three times late one hot August evening. Dyersville is known for baseball, but on that particular evening, no baseball or softball was played in the

By the middle of August, 1988 it was all over for me—or so I thought. After 68 days of shooting live action, the many miles of film were now ready for the tedious editing process back in Tinsel Town.

One fact that few people know is that the movie was titled "Shoeless Joe" until just two months before it was released. All filming and production was handled under this name. Back in Hollywood, Universal Studios researched the feasibility of the

a surprise since much of the community had become closely involved with the film and even had worn t-shirts emblazoned with the "Shoeless Joe" logo. (Director Phil Robinson fought bitterly saying the title would not stand on its own and really wanted to stay true to the book. In fact when Phil relayed this change to W.P. Kinsella, he was told that the original title had been "Dream Field." The title "Shoeless Joe" was created by the publishing company!) Everyone was looking forward to the

PHOTO BY DON LANSING

TWILIGHT SCENES TAKING SHAPE

PHOTO BY MELINDA SUE GORDON

BURT LANCASTER

Dyersville area as it was necessary to have as many lights as possible off to maintain darkness for the scene. There was only a 20-minute window of dusk to grab the best footage. The third take was a hit as instructions were broadcast over the radio waves from the whirlybird to have all cars toggle rapidly from low beam to high beam to project a twinkling effect that without words had a magical effect.

working title. Focus groups were brought into sessions and asked what the title "Shoeless Joe" brought to mind. Most who knew of Shoeless Joe figured it was an autobiography about the legendary ballplayer, while others figured it could be a homeless feature. In any case, to define the true storyline and to promote this film's true appeal, the title was changed to "Field of Dreams." Back in the Dyersville area, this came as

World Premiere being held at the Cinema 8 Theatres in Dubuque, Iowa on Thursday, April 20, 1989. It was a great success.

A few days later, the first visitor that I remember wandered onto my grounds. He was a curious looking guy, just standing there on my field looking a little dumb-founded to say the least. So I whispered to him a few questions. He said he was from

AMY MADIGAN & KEVIN COSTNER

THINGS TAKING SHAPE FOR THE "BOSTON" SCENE

New York and had just seen the movie. On his way back to California he wanted to stop by and see the place before it was gone. He just sat around for awhile, overlooking the place with a big old smile across his face and then headed back to his car.

THE FIRST VISITOR ARRIVED AT THE FIELD OF DREAMS ON MAY 5, 1989.

Before he left, I noticed that after a little talk with owner Don Lansing, he handed a New York Giants ballcap to the farmer. Don still has that cap today, but has never seen him back since. This one man started the wave of thousands who have gone the distance to see for themselves a piece of heaven on earth. A place where fantasy mixes with reality that has a special meaning to each person who visits the "Field of Dreams."

The Field

HISTORICAL VIEW CONTINUES ON THE NEXT PAGE.

DYERSVILLE, IOWA THEATER

BACKDROP PAINTING THAT WAS USED FOR SCENES IN TERENCE MANN'S APARTMENT

THE FIELD SPEAKS

CONTINUED HISTORY

Much has been documented since the day "Field of Dreams" hit the market back on April 21, 1989. As an Academy Award nominee for "Best Picture of the Year," thousands have personally stopped by to see this magical place on earth. Now, more than 30 years later, the "Field of Dreams" has become a baseball landmark in America—a sort of shrine to the great game of baseball. True to the simplicity and pristine quality that made the film so endearing, the "Field of Dreams Movie Site" has become a sort of living legend, playing its part in preserving a part of movie history for all who care to come out and experience it for themselves.

"FIELD OF DREAMS" HAS BEEN PLACED ON "PAUSE" FOR GENERATIONS TO COME.

PHOTO BY DON LANSING   THE FILM CREW

PHOTO BY DON LANSING   BEHIND THE SCENES AT THE FIELD

"FIELD OF DREAMS" HISTORICAL PHOTOGRAPHS AVAILABLE FOR VIEWING AND PURCHASE ONLINE FIELDOFDREAMSPHOTOS.COM

The result of a 1-hour 46-minute movie has put the "Field of Dreams" on "pause" for new generations to keep coming to see the place. Since so much has happened during the first 25 years, a summary of sorts will place us all in "real life rewind".

The next few pages highlight some old times from the past decades as they are relived in pictures and words for you to enjoy. Keep the dream alive!

PHOTO BY WENDOL JARVIS   JAPAN MOVIE PREMIER

HAS THE FILM HAD A LARGE INTERNATIONAL AUDIENCE?

Visitors have included people from as far away as Japan and Australia. Many successful American movies are released in other countries and "Field of Dreams" was no exception. Australia, Paris, Japan, London, Spain and Rio de Janeiro were the countries to host the film in their theaters. Japan's premier showing of "Field of Dreams" was much anticipated and became a box office hit in the land of the rising sun. Wendol Jarvis, Director of the Iowa Film Office, was responsible for pulling much of the January 18, 1990, event together. Full-blown marketing efforts in Japan captured the baseball-hungry interest of the people.

PHOTO BY MELINDA SUE GORDON   AMY MADIGAN TAKES A BREAK

WHO HAS VISITED THE FIELD OF DREAMS?

Everyone who has gone the distance to visit the Field is special in their own way. Some of the celebrities that have paid a visit are Reggie Jackson, George Brett, Sadahura Oh, Kirby Puckett, Lou Brock, WP Kinsella, Wade Boggs and Ernie Banks to name a few. On average, around 65,000 people a year visit. There is a guestbook available to sign your name and jot down your comments located right at the backstop.

PHOTO BY LOW AND INSIDE   HALL OF FAMER FERGUSON JENKINS

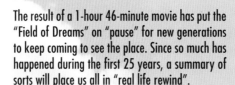

HAS THE FIELD OF DREAMS MOVIE SITE AFFECTED THE CITY OF DYERSVILLE?

Three letters shout YES. As a direct result of the Movie Site, several motels, restaurants and businesses have been established. The Dyersville Area Chamber of Commerce has grown as well. Road, water and sewer improvements have been completed all the way out to the Field of Dreams, which is nearly three miles out of the city.

WHAT DOES IT TAKE DURING THE YEAR TO KEEP THE FIELD OF DREAMS INTACT?

The Lansing farm has been voted by Briggs and Stratton as one of the "Top 10 Lawns in the Country" if you can imagine, so landscaping chores on the two acres do take on a special

PHOTO BY STEPHEN GASSMAN

meaning for the crew. An underground sprinkler system was added to keep the grass looking playable all summer long. Several improvements have been made to the grounds, including a new retaining wall under the white picket fence. During an average week, it takes about 30 hours to keep everything in place.

DOES SOMEONE STILL LIVE IN THE FAMOUS HOUSE?

Yes - up until 2018. One of the owners of Go The Distance Baseball, LLC, lived on-site to help maintain the property which is now available for public tours and overnight rental to enjoy.

PHOTO BY STEPHEN GASSMAN

PHOTO BY MELINDA SUE GORDON

PHOTO BY LOW AND INSIDE   JERRY & LYNN RYAN MARRIED AT HOME PLATE 1989

HAS ANYONE BEEN MARRIED AT THE "FIELD OF DREAMS?"

Jerry and Lynn Ryan from Rochester, NY were the first couple to wed at home plate in 1989. Betrothed interested in renting my grounds for their very special event should email me at info@fodmoviesite.com for rental details.

WHO ORIGINALLY OWNED THE LEFT FIELD PORTION OF THE "FIELD OF DREAMS?"

A neighboring farmer Al Ameskamp owned this portion of the Field. In fact, soon after the film was released, Al was planting corn and came to the spot where his portion of the Field had been carved out. After several hours of internal debate, he decided to replant corn. Eventually, due to public outcry, Al rebuilt the left field portion of the Field.

PHIL AND KEVIN GO OVER SOME DETAILS DURING THE SHOOT

WAS ANYONE IN THE LANSING FAMILY ACTUALLY IN THE FILM?

Don Lansing, Don's mother, sisters Mary Lou, Carol, Betty and her husband Jim, along with many nieces and nephews were extras in different scenes.

To be an extra you had to fill out an application and send a picture of yourself. The production crew would call a couple of days in advance to see if you were available to show up. You were required to bring three changes of clothes, no bright colors. You may have been on location a few hours or possibly all day long depending on how filming was going. Extras were paid $50 a day.

The Dubuque Area Chamber of Commerce and
The Iowa Department of Economic Development
Department invite you to the World Premiere
Showing and Champagne Reception of

FIELD OF DREAMS

Date: Thursday, April 20, 1989
Time: 7:00 p.m.
Location: Excellence Cinema Center 8 Theatres
Reception: Best Western Dubuque Inn
RSVP with check by April 14, 1989

Scenes the Lansing family members appeared in were: the school gym, PTA meeting on banning of books; nosey neighbors along the road when the corn was being cut to build the ballfield and the last scene in the movie when cars were all coming. Don was in the first car, his mother and sister Betty were in the second car, Rita and Al Ameskamp the third car, and Don's sisters Mary Lou and Carol in the fourth car.

Also there were neighbors and other local towns-people in the movie.

THE FIELD SPEAKS
CONTINUED HISTORY

ARE THERE CERTAIN THINGS WITHIN THE PROPERTY THAT ARE DIFFERENT THAN BEFORE FILMING?

The swing was rented from a family in Dubuque and had to be returned after filming was completed. A replacement was found to closely match the previous "star". There is a souvenir stand designed to resemble the barns as it blends into the farm background. Several trees were relocated for filming. Efforts are made to keep the movie site intact.

PHOTO BY LOW AND INSIDE   **HALL OF FAMER GEORGE BRETT**

Upper Deck sponsored a much larger event within the city of Dyersville, complete with a Celebrity Baseball Game at the Field of Dreams. This too, was held over the Labor Day Weekend and names such as players above mixed with Hollywood actors Dwier Brown, Bruce Boxleitner, Meat Loaf, Jason Priestly, and Rhonda Shear among others.

The following years a Labor Day Festival was held within Dyersville and players such as George Brett, Lou Brock, Jimmy Wynn were part of this era. During one of these Labor Day Weekend events, a

PHOTO BY LOW AND INSIDE   **LOU BROCK, REGGIE JACKSON & BOB GIBSON**

"Sermon on the Mound" was given by Terry Rush of Tulsa, Oklahoma, much to the delight of many who listened to him that bright Sunday morning.

HAS THE FIELD OF DREAMS BEEN USED FOR FILMING SINCE THE MOVIE?

The biggest production was called "Dreamfield" put together by ESPN a few years ago which included narration by James Earl Jones. This was a look back at the wave of cars that continue to come to visit the Movie Site long after the film was released. Other video productions have included commercials for television by Wheaties promoting their frosted cereal product. The late Kirby Puckett had filmed a baseball promotional video for a campaign to build a new stadium in Minnesota and to capture footage for his retirement weekend celebration in 1996. "MLB Network" filmed the opening intro segment for the 2013 MLB League Division Series, titled "Field of Dreamers" which was nominated for three Sports Emmys.

PHOTO BY STEPHEN GASSMAN   **WINTER BLUES**

WHAT ORGANIZED EVENTS HAVE BEEN STAGED AT THE "FIELD OF DREAMS?"

In 1991 a baseball fantasy camp and "The First Competitive Baseball Game" was held on Labor Day. Charity tickets were sold as hundreds of people showed up to see old time ballplayers such as Reggie Jackson, Lou Brock, Curt Flood, Bob Feller and more turn out to play some ball. Then in 1992,

PHOTO BY LOW AND INSIDE   **JASON PRIESTLY**

PHOTO BY LOW AND INSIDE   **REGGIE JACKSON UNLOADS!**

PHOTO BY KEVIN J. KAPP   **KIRBY PUCKETT TAKES A STROLL OUT FROM THE CORN 1996**

FIELD OF DREAMS GLOWING INTO MIDNIGHT

I'VE HEARD "IS THIS HEAVEN? NO IT'S IOWA" ALL OVER THE PLACE. DID THEY GET THAT FROM SOMEWHERE?

It is from the book "Shoeless Joe" and was used in the movie. W.P. Kinsella gave his blessing to the state for use of the slogan penned in Iowa City, Iowa back in 1978. It has proved to be a popular state slogan, unmatched in the Iowa's state history.

AREN'T SEVERAL SLOGANS FROM "FIELD OF DREAMS" USED IN MARKETING?

Advertising and art industries worldwide have adopted some of the now famous slogans such as: "IF YOU BUILD IT," "FIELD OF DREAMS,""IS THIS HEAVEN?" and "GO THE DISTANCE" just to name a few. The movie has a strong community-oriented theme and is open ended to apply to many different scenarios. For whatever the reason, these phrases have become an integral part of America's identity worldwide.

RAY LIOTTA (SHOELESS JOE), JAMES EARL JONES (TERENCE MANN), KEVIN COSTNER (RAY KINESELLA), AMY MADIGAN (ANNIE KINSELLA)

CONFERENCE AT THE MOUND?

FAMILY TIME AT THE FIELD OF DREAMS

When the filmmakers left the "Field of Dreams," they left behind more than the bleachers and baselines. They left memories and magic and the friendships they had formed during a scorching summer sun. Among the thousands who participated in the film were many outstanding baseball players who had suited up to create the illusion of

PHOTO BY LOW AND INSIDE   **GHOST SUNDAY**

a team. They pitched and hit the balls and then ran the bases alongside the stars of the film, including Kevin Costner, Ray Liotta, and James Earl Jones. The filmmakers closed the sets, packed their gear, and sold off the used uniforms and equipment.

> ## "THIS IS MY MOST SPECIAL PLACE IN ALL THE WORLD, RAY. ONCE A PLACE TOUCHES YOU LIKE THIS, THE WIND NEVER BLOWS SO COLD AGAIN. YOU FEEL FOR IT, LIKE IT WAS YOUR CHILD."
>
> Dr. Archibald "Moonlight" Graham from "Field of Dreams"

A year later, the movie's fans started visiting the "Field of Dreams" to find their mystical moments at the preserved movie site. A mere trickle soon turned into a steady stream of pilgrims seeking the magic. One day that sultry summer, a local neighbor of "Field of Dreams," Keith Rahe, wanted to

embellish the experience for the tourists by donning the pinstripes and strolling through a cornfield beyond the "Field of Dreams." The guys decided to give it a go, not knowing that among the spectators was a reporter for the "Cedar Rapids Gazette." The next weekend there was a

PHOTO BY LOW AND INSIDE   **DENISE STILLMAN, GHOST SUNDAY SMILES**

story about these guys coming out of the cornfield and by Sunday afternoon there were hundreds of people waiting to see the Ghosts return.

"ONE-PART BASEBALL AND TWO-PARTS VAUDVILLE."

Los Angeles Times, Beverly Beyette; Ghost Player Review

Soon what had been a random action turned into a dedicated team of former semi-professional and professional baseball players who came to the field for "Ghost Player Sundays." The men would play catch, sign autographs, and pose for photos to the delight of the fans. Soon pick-up games turned into a full-blown comedy routine and sports skills camps for the young fans. Their baseball clinics were well respected and the comedy show gained the nick-name, the "Greatest Show on Dirt". The appearances at the Field led to a worldwide tour through 26 countries over the years promoting baseball and "Field of Dreams." The Ghost Players have led parades, toured hospitals and orphanages, and even attended baseball legend Ozzie Smith's (St. Louis Cardinals), retirement party. They have played ball with the US Military All-Star Baseball Team and have been featured in the documentaries: "Dreamfield: The Field of Dreams Story" (ESPN) and "Ghost Player: Relive the Magic."

PHOTO BY LOW AND INSIDE   **KEITH RAHE, GHOSTPLAYERS FOUNDER**

During the past 30+ years, the Ghost Players have traveled to 26 countries and even more US Military bases around the globe and yet they prefer the joy of playing to the home crowd.

The original eight-player team has expanded to over 30 members over the 30+ years they have performed. Most of the original players can still be found strapping on their cleats to get the chance to share in the joy of playing baseball at the "Field of Dreams." They also have been involved with MLB and "Roberto's Kids Foundation" in Puerto Rico.

By Suzie Wright, DreamCatcher Productions LLC

PHOTO BY LOW AND INSIDE   **DANCING GHOSTPLAYERS**

"DREAMFIELD: The Field of Dreams Story" (ESPN)

"GHOST PLAYER: Relive The Magic" (DreamCatcher Productions)
ISBN: 978-0984087815   www.GhostPlayer.us
View "GHOST PLAYER: Relive The Magic" on Amazon Prime and SaltboxTV.com

"TRAVELS WITH GHOSTS AND OTHER TALES" BOOK
ISBN: 978-0984087808   www.GhostPlayer.us

GHOST PLAYER ARCHIVE: archive.org/details/ghostplayers
501(c)(3) non-profit that was founded to build an internet library. Its purposes include offering permanent access for researchers, historians, scholars, people with disabilities and the general public to historical collections that exist in digital format.

PHOTO BY LOW AND INSIDE   **MARV MAIERS, LEGENDARY GHOSTPLAYER**

WANNA HAVE A CATCH?
WITH DWIER BROWN

It is often said that during certain critical moments in your life, time seems to stand still. The final scene of "Field of Dreams" is definitely one of those instances. Everything leading up to the final 5-minutes of the film, where Ray Kinsella is given his second chance with his dad (John Kinsella, played by Dwier Brown) has hit home with audiences worldwide for over 25 years. Like a pitcher with 2-outs and a full count in the bottom of the 9th inning, Dwier Brown delivers the final strike to win the ballgame — of life.

PHOTO BY MELINDA SUE GORDON   RAY AND JOHN KINSELLA SEE EYE TO EYE

Growing up on a farm in Sharon Center, Ohio, Dwier Brown played Little League, cheered on the Cleveland Indians and loved Roberto Clemente. He went out for baseball at Highland High School, but didn't find his name on the list to make the team. He told a friend that day that his coach would regret that decision and that one day his photo would be in Cooperstown, NY, at the National Baseball Hall of Fame. Life rolled on and theater groups and acting workshops took center stage.

PHOTO BY DWIER BROWN   GHOSTPLAYERS ON SET DURING FILMING JULY 1988

Dwier began his acting career in the early 80s with roles in various films and television shows. Dwier pitched for "Field of Dreams" in May of 1988 and heard he got the role to play John Kinsella, that was scheduled to shoot three days in July. In June of 1988, Dwier received word from family that his father was very ill. Although he already had tickets to fly home, Dwier ended up changing it to an earlier date, listening to the gut feeling he had. Dwier is thankful to have done this, and arrived in time to spend the last few hours his dad had on this earth.

In a whirlwind of emotions, Dwier reported to the set in Dyersville, Iowa in July as scheduled for his three-day shoot. This scene turned into two weeks

PHOTO BY DWIER BROWN   ART LAFLUER, DWIER BROWN, STEVE EASTIN, CHARLES HOYES

of shooting in 15-minute segments to take advantage of the golden light (magic hour) just after sunset. Dwier stated that he hadn't had time to accept that his father was gone, and felt as though his dad was right there in the cornfields during filming. The addition of the word 'Dad' to the film before 'wanna have a catch' was done after audience screenings of the film.

Time stood still.

"THE FIELD OF DREAMS MOVIE SITE IS A PLACE WHERE YOU REALLY CAN'T HIDE FROM ANYTHING."

Personal Observation by Dwier Brown

In the 25 years since, Dwier has stopped back at the Field on a few occasions. He applauds that the Movie Site has been kept the way it was with minimal changes made. When asked what his hopes are for "Field of Dreams" and the Movie Site, Dwier says, "the film is going to do whatever it's going to do. I'm grateful that people talk about it as this generation's 'It's A Wonderful Life.' As for

PHOTO BY LOW AND INSIDE   BRIAN FRANKISH, DWIER BROWN, DON LANSING 04.23.2014

the Movie Site, it's great seeing young people there and nice to see that a new generation is being introduced to a sweet film that kids should see."

What is it about baseball and the "Field of Dreams" that's so magical? Dwier quickly responds, "I think baseball is a slower game than most other sports. So much mental work is going on during a game between pitches with hitters, base coaches, catchers, dugout signals and so on. To the untrained eye, it's boring and slow. Frequently our relationships with our dads are based on a lot of unspoken things, much like the game of baseball. Playing catch is so profound, because it wordlessly mimics what we do with our fathers. I give to you (throwing) and I get from you (catching) which symbolizes a deep level of meaning. In baseball you can stay there a long time to satisfy a need for exchange, when words don't always work."

PHOTO BY MELINDA SUE GORDON   JOHN KINSELLA (DWIER BROWN) ON SET 1988

Dwier has made his dreams come true. He has authored a book titled "If You Build It.." which shares many stories and thoughts about father and son relationships. "Finding the true meaning of my own relationship with my father was a by-product of this process, which was a surprise to me," says Dwier. "Meeting so many dads out there who have shared their stories continues to be inspiring. It is amazing that a specific character such as John Kinsella, can be such a universal touchstone to people," he concludes.

PHOTO BY LAURIE BROWN   KEVIN COSTNER & DWIER 04.21.2014

They say art imitates life at times. In The National Baseball Hall of Fame in Cooperstown, NY, a photo of Dwier Brown (John Kinsella) hangs on display for all to see, for generations to come who have gone the distance. Time stood still, and Dwier Brown, wondered, "Is this Heaven?"

By Nick Vetter, Low and Inside LLC

"IF YOU BUILD IT..." ISBN# 978-0996057103
FOR MORE INFORMATION VISIT: WWW.DWIERBROWN.COM

Ideas and dreams are a very powerful force in the world. Generations have flourished on new ideas and inventions. There once was a woman by the name of Denise Miarecki Stillman who followed her heart and went after those dreams. Her group purchased the Field of Dreams Movie Site from the Lansings in 2012 with big ideas for a large youth baseball complex named All Star Ballpark Heaven. She also had visions of the first ever MLB game in Iowa to be held at the Field of Dreams which came true on August 12, 2021 with over 7,800 fans and was broadcast live on national television. The Chicago White Sox defeated the New York Yankees 9-8 in a classic old-school baseball game.

PHOTO BY LOW AND INSIDE
DENISE STILLMAN PLAQUE UNVEILED JUNE 15, 2019

PHOTO BY LOW AND INSIDE
SUE REIDEL WHO FOUND THE LANSING FARM FOR HOLLYWOOD FILMING REFLECTING ON 25th FOD ANNIVERSARY JUNE 14, 2014

PHOTO BY LOW AND INSIDE   **DENISE STILLMAN & MLB COMMISSIONER ROB MANFRED**

PHOTO BY LOW AND INSIDE
DYERSVILLE MAYOR ALVIN HAAS DENISE STILLMAN KEY TO THE CITY JUNE 14, 2014

PHOTO BY LOW AND INSIDE
DENISE MIARECKI STILLMAN & MLB COMMISSIONER ROB MANFRED MAY 26, 2016

PHOTO BY LOW AND INSIDE
KEVIN COSTNER & DWIER BROWN RECREATING THE FINAL CATCH SCENE DURING THE 25th FOD ANNIVERSARY JUNE 14, 2014

The Field of Dreams 25th Anniversary Celebration took place on June 14, 2014 with Kevin Costner returning along with a whole cast of Hollywood stars and Major League players for the event. There are various photos on the inside covers of this book that show several different angles of the excitement that happened on this sacred ground in Iowa.

On September 30, 2019 the Field of Dreams Movie Site was sold to This is Heaven LLC, a group headed by Hall of Famer, Frank Thomas. On April 14, 2022 they hit the ground running and announced an $80 million expansion plan at the Field of Dreams to include several ballfields, hotel, fieldhouse and amphitheater. See rendering image on next page. Dyersville city water, sewer and utilities are already in motion after a lengthy legal delay paving the way for All Star Ballpark Heaven complex to be completed in stages by 2025.

If you build it... Dreams can come true.

By Nick Vetter, Low and Inside LLC

PHOTO BY LOW AND INSIDE
KEVIN COSTNER & BOB COSTAS INTERVIEW DURING THE 25th FOD ANNIVERSARY JUNE 14, 2014

PHOTO BY LOW AND INSIDE   **MLB COMMISSIONER ROB MANFRED & DENISE STILLMAN**

MLB started the National Baseball Hall of Fame traveling exhibit at the Field of Dreams Movie Site on May 26, 2016. MLB Commissioner Rob Manfred was on hand and also met with Denise Miarecki Stillman to discuss her vision (see various photos) for All Star Ballpark Heaven and a future MLB game at the Field of Dreams.

PHOTO BY LOW AND INSIDE
DENISE MIARECKI PLAQUE UNVEILED JUNE 15, 2019 DENISE'S FAMILY & CHILDREN SHARED THE HONOR

PHOTO BY LOW AND INSIDE
TIMOTHY BUSFIELD, KEVIN COSTNER, BOB COSTAS FILMING DURING THE 25th FOD ANNIVERSARY JUNE 14, 2014

PHOTO BY LOW AND INSIDE   **THE NEW MLB BALLFIELD BEING EXCAVATED**

PHOTO BY LOW AND INSIDE   **KEVIN COSTNER PREGAME SPEECH BEFORE THE WHITE SOX VS YANKEES GAME ON AUGUST 12, 2021**

PHOTO BY LOW AND INSIDE   **KEVIN COSTNER PREGAME ENTRY TO MLB FIELD DURING THE WHITE SOX VS YANKEES GAME ON AUGUST 12, 2021**

PHOTO BY LOW AND INSIDE   **KEVIN COSTNER PREGAME SPEECH BEFORE THE WHITE SOX VS YANKEES GAME ON AUGUST 12, 2021**

PHOTO BY LOW AND INSIDE   **KEVIN COSTNER & FANS AT THE FIELD OF DREAMS 25TH ANNIVERSARY CELEBRATION ON JUNE 14, 2014**

PHOTO BY LOW AND INSIDE   **PANORAMIC VIEW OF THE NEW MLB BALLFIELD AND THE ORIGINAL FIELD OF DREAMS FARM AND MOVIE SITE BALLFIELD**

PHOTO BY LOW AND INSIDE   **WALK-OFF HOMERUN WIN FOR WHITE SOX WIN ON AUGUST 12, 2021**

PHOTO BY LOW AND INSIDE   **MLB PLAQUE INSTALLED IN 2021**

PHOTO BY LOW AND INSIDE   **PLAY BALL! FIRST MLB GAME IN IOWA HISTORY – WHITE SOX VS YANKEES GAME ON AUGUST 12, 2021**

IF YOU BUILD IT EXHIBIT
Located in Dyersville, Iowa
IFYOUBUILDITEXHIBIT.COM
Facebook: If You Build It Exhibit

PHOTO BY LOW AND INSIDE   **GHOST PLAYER MURAL IN DYERSVILLE IA**

FIELD OF DREAMS SITE PLAN RELEASED APRIL 14, 2022

19

W.P. KINSELLA
AUTHOR COMBINES MAGIC AND REALITY

PHOTO BY DON LANSING

he often indulged in his favorite whim of traveling across the U.S. and Canada attending baseball games. His self-belief in his writing and hard work have paid off. This author of baseball folklore sums it up quite well with this overview as told to the Globe and Mail, "The secret of a fiction writer is to make the dull interesting by imagination and embellishment, and to tone down the bizarre until it is believable. Stories or novels are not about events, but about the people that events happen to," Kinsella concludes.

"I DON'T PLAY THE GAME; IN FACT I THROW LIKE A GIRL!"

This writing champ has shared his imagination with those of us who care to dream and has showed many that he has a style all his own.

By Willie Steele   Sources: Contemporary Authors and a thanks to "Doctor Baseball," Peter Bjarkman for his personal insight on W.P. Kinsella. W.P. Kinsella died on September 16, 2016.

BOOKS BY KINSELLA

Dance Me Outside
Scars
Born Indian
Shoeless Joe
The Ballad of the Public Trustee
The Moccasin Telegraph
The Thrill of the Grass
The Alligator Report
The Iowa Baseball Confederacy
Five Stories
The Fencepost Chronicles
Billy in Trinidad
Red Wolf, Red Wolf
Touching the Bases
Butterfly Winter
If Wishes Were Horses
Box Socials
The Winter Helen Stopped By
If Wishes Were Horses
Magic Time
The Dixon Cornbelt League
Baseball Fantastic
Japanese Baseball & Other Stories

William Patrick Kinsella leads the league in a different category. He doesn't have the highest on-base percentage or even most times hit by a pitch. W.P. Kinsella is dominantly the best short-story baseball writer in the world. His style is truly one-of-a-kind which combines both magic and reality together on the pages of his growing number of baseball volumes.

PHOTO BY DON LANSING

"Shoeless Joe," from which the movie "Field of Dreams" was derive, was a 25-page story selected to appear in an anthology entitled Aurora: New Canadian Writers 1979. His words were in front of the right eyes one day and an editor at Houghton Mifflin (publisher) saw the story. He contacted Kinsella and asked him about expanding the story into a novel.

W.P.'s response to the call, "I had never written anything over 25 pages, but if you want to work with me, I'll try it. To my surprise they accepted. I left the story intact and used it as the first chapter, then built on the plot with a variety of other material. I enjoyed doing it very much. They were such wonderful characters I'd created, and I liked being audacious in another way. I put in no sex, violence, no obscenity, none of that stuff that sells. I wanted to write a book for imaginative readers, an affirmative statement about life. I've mixed in so much, I'm not sure what's real and what's not, but as long as you can convince people you know what you're talking about, it doesn't matter. If you're convincing, they'll believe it."

With this category leader, where did the love for baseball begin? W.P. Kinsella's father played some minor league ball and talked about it quite often. Kinsella is quoted: "I never played or saw a game until I was eleven years old. I loved it as a spectator. I don't play the game; in fact I throw like a girl!"

His lyrical descriptions about the game in his work undoubtedly evidence his knowledge of baseball. Kinsella goes on to say, "I'm not a fanatic. It may appear so, but I'm not. My feeling for baseball is a little like Cordelia's statement to King Lear. She said she loved him as a daughter loves a father. No more and no less."

Kinsella, who was born on May 25, 1935 in Edmonton, Alberta (Canada) attended and taught at the University of Iowa in the 70s, loved the state. In fact, as a Society of Baseball Research member,

1935 – 2016

AGAIN$T THE ODD$

THE LEGEND OF SHOELESS JOE JACKSON

American history is laced with stories of adventure by those who have risked everything. Some who have reached for the sky have fallen short while others were able to grab hold of a few stars. Those select few, who are characterized as "legends" in the history books, live on in spirit long after leaving this world behind. Shoeless Joe Jackson was a man who's legendary story continues to intrigue us yet today in America.

Joseph Jefferson Jackson was born July 16, 1887, in Pickens County, SC. The Civil War had ended some time before, but the rebuilding of America was a ways off yet. To make a living, the Jackson family had moved to Pelzer, SC, to work in the largest textile mill in the United States. At the age of 6, Joe went to work at the textile mill and never really had the chance to get an education due to the long and deafening hours put in at the mill. Workers at the mill were from many different backgrounds, speaking in many different dialects and making it difficult to comprehend what life was really all about. This was the norm for all families, and their main recreational outlet was playing baseball on Saturday afternoons. These games were unorganized battles, for the most part. The mills would usually have a ballfield and other community fixtures on the premises for their workers to use. Joe grew up in this atmosphere and developed a great interest in the game of "base."

TEXTILE BASEBALL

"Time went by and the industrial cotton mills were largely responsible for the South's recovery from the Civil War. Collectively, the mills brought the 'true grit' American working class together. The timeless competitive spirit of work and play, from scratch to scrap teams, evolved into a baseball era of unyielding aspiration and desire to excel. Textile baseball produced many great legendary ball players. Mill workers by the thousands once swarmed out of drudgery, when the whistles blew on Saturday afternoons, to their village ballparks to enjoy the thrill of America's favorite past time—BASEBALL."

FROM GROWING UP WITH SHOELESS JOE BY JOE THOMPSON

"AGAINST THE ODDS" STORY CONTINUES ON THE NEXT PAGE...

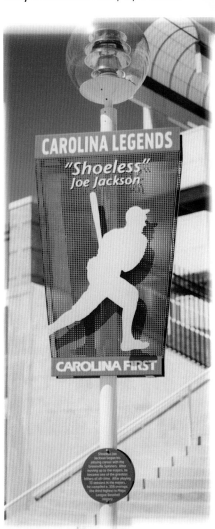

PHOTO BY DURHAM HUNT   **SIGN AT THE BI LO CENTER IN GREENVILLE, SC**

PHOTO BY STEPHEN GASSMAN

PHOTO BY LOW AND INSIDE

23

The Jackson family moved back to West Greenville, SC, for work at the new Brandon Mill, and Joe, who was only 13, quickly became a regular player for the Brandon Mill team. The Major League scouts were soon monitoring his every at bat, and in 1908, Joe began his professional career with the Philadelphia Athletics.

Leaving Greenville to follow his dream was one of the toughest things Joe had ever done. In fact, 100 miles into the train ride, during a layover in Charlotte, Joe ran off the train and hitched a ride back to his home. Three days later, he was convinced by Connie Mack, manager of the A's, to fulfill his obligation to join the team in Philadelphia. Mack even sent one his star players to Greenville to make sure of this! After several short stints in the minor leagues, Joe was ready for the big leagues. Joe Jackson immediately established himself as one of baseball's premier hitters when he was traded to Cleveland.

PHOTO BY DURHAM HUNT

JOE JACKSON'S LIQUOR STORE IN GREENVILLE; THE SHOP WITH TWO WINDOWS AND A DOOR

WHERE DID THE NICKNAME "SHOELESS" COME FROM?

Everyone wonders how Joe got tagged with the legendary nickname "Shoeless" Joe Jackson. It is

break them in before he was called up to the Major Leagues later that year. But the first time he wore these new leather spikes - June 6 at Greenville's Memminger Street Park against the Anderson Electricians - they gave him blisters. Around the 5th inning, Joe took them off. He played the rest of the game in his stocking feet. While he was out in the outfield, no one really noticed. But in the bottom of the 7th, Joe came to the plate with his team down 1 and hit the longest home run in the history of the park. As he rounded 3rd on his home run trot, an Anderson fan yelled, "You shoeless son-of-a-gun!"

paper in the country had run the story about the "shoeless wonder from South Carolina." He's been know as "Shoeless Joe" ever since.

WHAT'S THE REAL STORY OF THE "BLACK BETSY" BAT?

The bat was turned by a local woodworker and fan of Joe's named Charlie Ferguson, who made the bat out of the northern side of a hickory tree. "Black Betsy" weighed in at 48 ounces, and was Joe's favorite bat, but it broke early in Joe's Major League career. Nicknames stuck around, though, as writers in this era created an identity for many of the ballplayers they wrote about in their columns. There was no radio or television, so the pictures painted by writers were eagerly anticipated by fans every day. While writers still referred to Joe's bat(s) as "Black Betsy," he was actually using custom-made Louisville Sluggers which weighed 39 ounces each from 1911 to 1920. In July of 1920, Joe gave one as a gift to Babe Ruth, who then gave Joe one of his. In fact, Babe Ruth is quoted as saying, "I liked Joe Jackson's hitting style and, with his help, I copied it." Even Ty Cobb said he thought Joe was "the greatest natural hitter I ever saw." Joe Jackson's home runs were known as "Saturday Specials" after his showmanship during the Textile League games. Recently, "Black Betsy" was rediscovered in the possession of Lester Erwin, who received it after Katie Jackson died. It sold at auction in 2001 for $577,610.

PHOTO COURTESY OF JOE ANDERS

JACKSON TALKING BALL WITH THE BOYS; RALPH HARBIN, SHOELESS JOE JACKSON, HARRY FOSTER, JOE ANDERS

by far one of the most well-known nicknames in America still today. The origin of this event dates back to 1908 when Joe was a member of the Greenville Spinners of the Class D Carolina League. Joe had bought a new pair of cleats. He wanted to

Carter "Scoop" Latimer, a 14-year old beat reporter for The Greenville News, was sitting near the wild fan and overheard the remark. He laughed and wrote it down in his notepard. He put it in the paper the next day, and within two weeks, every

Shoeless Joe had one of the strongest throwing arms a ballplayer could possess. Proof of this is engraved on a trophy he won on September 17, 1917, at a Boston All Star Benefit game. During a pre-game carnival show, an All Star throwing contest was held. Jackson took first place with a throw that measured 396 feet 8 inches! Babe Ruth won a fungo hitting contest. On other occasions,

Joe was seen tossing the ball well over 400 feet. Joe Jackson, who stood 6'1" and weighed a solid 200 pounds was considered to be the most versatile and natural athlete baseball had to offer.

Baseball, during the early 1900s, was rife with corruption. Betting was prevalent during the Dead Ball Era, and players often threw at bats, games, series, or even complete seasons for a little extra cash. The gangster era was a reality in American culture, and with so many players feeling they were underpaid by their owners, they often took things into their own hands to make money during their careers. There is speculation that the World Series of 1905, 1912, and 1918 were all thrown, which paved the way for the powerhouse team of 1919, the Chicago White Sox, to consider doing the same. Chicago had one of the strongest clubs in baseball history and were in the midst of a dynasty, having won it all in 1917.

In 1919, the Chicago White Sox found themselves in a battle with the Cincinnati Reds for the World's Series. It was to be a best of nine series. Odds were 5-1 that the Sox would take the crown again.

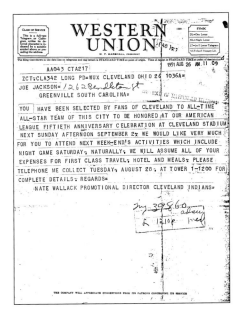

Rumors were everywhere about the "fix" on the World's Series of 1919 and everyone had their own take on what was fact and what was fiction. Charles Comiskey commented during the season, "To me baseball is as honorable as any other business. It has to be, or it would not last out a season... Crookedness and baseball do not mix... This year, 1919, is the greatest season of them all."

The rumors finally died down after the 1919 Series. But during the 1920 season, other players soon realized the financial advantages of playing along with gamblers. Rumors began surfacing again regarding other "fixed" games, specifically a Cubs/Phillies three-game series. In September

Today he is but a whisper in the wind,
But he is truly one of the best there has ever been.
We all know his name, it was Shoeless Joe,
And this is the way his story did go.
Most remember his stint with the notorious Black Sox,
But to find out the truth we must turn back the clocks.
His name came to be on a day his feet did hurt,
So he decided to go barefoot and play in the dirt.
Not a soul did notice until a close third base play,
When a fan yelled, "Hey, it's Shoeless Joe!" and the name did stay.
An extremely gifted player, he could hit, catch, and run,
But he lacked education and character, you could say he was dumb.
The A's were his first team, and of all the players it was him they mocked,
So he was traded to Cleveland where he was treated like a jock.
It was for them this natural hitter would show his grand slap,
He was without error on the field and never took a nap.
Joe improved his accurate arm and ran the bases with speed,
Soon he became the type of player every team did need.
So it wasn't lack of knowledge or slightly by chance,
That even Babe Ruth patterned himself after Jackson's stance.
But then hard times hit Cleveland, they had an empty shoe box,
So in 1915, Joe was traded to the White Sox.
For $31,500 and three players unknown,
Chicago came to be Joe's final major league home.
He hit his weight for the Sox, but still reigned as their star,
With the team Comiskey gathered, Shoeless Joe was on par.
In 1920 he hit .392 and had one of his best seasons,
But it was that same year everything crashed due to scandalous reasons.
Friends pleaded his Series' average .375 proved he played square,
But the $5-G's in Joe's pocket showed Landis he was there.
The young fans were upset and cried, "Say it ain't so!",
Still the Commissioner played hardball and said, "Joe, you gotta go."
Banned from baseball for life, he returned to his South Carolina hometown,
Started a dry cleaning business, but you can't keep a good man down!
He could still be found swinging "Black Betsy", his forever famed bat,
After all, in a sandlot or a ballpark was where his heart was at.
In time his dignity was restored, if not his due glory,
But it was in 1951 he passed on, and ended this story.
So fly high in the sky, you legend of time,
You're far from forgotten, you're still on our mind...

1920, a Cook County (Chicago) grand jury was put together to look into the rumors and the probe soon widened to include the 1919 World's Series.

The team owners took action and dissolved the three-man National Commission run by Ban Johnson who had overseen Major League Baseball. A one-man position was created—the independent commissioner. Judge Kenesaw Mountain Landis

PHOTO BY DURHAM HUNT   SHOELESS JOE JACKSON'S HOME NOW IS A MUSEUM

was appointed because he had a reputation for being able to stand on his own and commanded respect. Landis' attitude about baseball was summarized in this classic statement: "Baseball is something more than a game to an American boy, it is the training field for life work. Destroy his faith in its squareness and honesty and you have destroyed something more; you have planted suspicion of all things in his heart."

The Sox were again in contention for the 1920 pennant when the grand jury began calling players and gamblers alike to the stand about what had happened during the previous season finale. All eight ballplayers that were originally identified were indicted for conspiracy to defraud the public and injure the business of Charles Comiskey along with the American League. However, there was not an Illinois statute against throwing a game or even arranging to have one fixed.

"BASEBALL IS MORE THAN A NATIONAL GAME, IT IS AN AMERICAN INSTITUTION."

The grand jury summarized what the public felt quite well while evaluating evidence against those involved in baseball's worst scandal. Their perspective was expressed by the jury foreman, "Baseball is more than a national game, it is an American institution. [Our great teacher of] respect for proper authority, self-confidence, fair-mindedness, quick judgement and self-control."

Before the trial, the newly-appointed Commissioner of baseball, Kenesaw Mountain Landis, said if the players were to be found not guilty, they would all be allowed back in MLB. The jury found all eight players not guilty. The day after the verdict was announced, Landis barred all eight men from baseball for life anyway, claiming guilt by association with the involvement to some degree for "fixing" games. After announcing his decision, Landis said, "The only thing in anybody's mind now is to make baseball what the millions of fans throughout the United States want it to be." The rumors had created skepticism among fans and the future of baseball was at stake. The outcome of the "Black Sox Scandal" is recorded in American history as the scheme that rocked the very foundations of baseball.

Shoeless Joe Jackson ended his 13-year career with a lifetime .356 batting average, which remains fourth best in history. He was a legendary ballplayer, and few have been compared to him ever since.

Life after MLB changed for Joe and his wife, Katie, but the sport remained a steady part of his "diet." There are less than a dozen known instances of Joe playing under assumed names – though they did happen. Joe played on several Southern outlaw teams, and was even rumored to play in Dubuque, Iowa at one point. Joe then opened a dry cleaning business in Savannah, and owned a liquor store in his hometown of Greenville, SC. He played ball

PHOTO BY DURHAM HUNT   BRANDON BAPTIST CHURCH

again for several of the mills in the area and enjoyed talking baseball with the kids outside his liquor store. It was next to the hangout of the day—the drug store.

Joe Anders was one of the youngsters whom "Shoeless Joe" Jackson took under his wing. Anders went to the liquor store one day and introduced himself to Jackson. They were both

PHOTO BY DURHAM HUNT   SHOELESS JOE JACKSON PARK AT BRANDON MILL

from the Brandon Mill community in West Greenville, and even started their careers on the exact same ballfield. This common thread sparked a friendship that went far beyond baseball. Joe taught him how to properly hold the bat along with other skills to make this young ballplayer better with practice. Many days Jackson would show up at the ballfield and talk ball with the kids along with providing all of them with fountain drinks and ice cream from the drug store. Community involvement with the kids was sort of Jackson's way of keeping the baseball blues away.

SHOELESS JOE JACKSON ENDED HIS 13-YEAR CAREER WITH A LIFETIME .356 BATTING AVERAGE

Looking back, Joe Anders, who was a star player for Brandon Mills during his playing days, has many great memories. "I don't remember Joe Jackson as the great ballplayer but as the great man that he was. He was just that kind of man. Any kid from that group would tell you the exact same thing. He didn't talk about the scandal with me, but he did say that he missed baseball. He was hurt, you could tell. I never heard him say anything bitter about the game of baseball. He loved the game, and did tell me that he was innocent."

"The old timers would always stop in and see Shoeless when in the area," Anders went on to say. "I remember one day, Jackson called to me, 'Come here Good Buddy' (what Jackson always called me), and introduced Ty Cobb to me as 'the greatest hitter of all time.' Cobb quickly pinned the title back to Jackson. Ty also told me that Shoeless Joe could hit the dead ball longer than Babe Ruth could hit the live ball!"

As with every other aspect of life in America today, baseball has become a complex blend of business, entertainment and commercialism. Anders looks back and remembers the many times Jackson would show 'Black Betsy' to the kids. With all the time spent with Jackson, Joe Anders never even got an autograph from his hero. "I guess I didn't really think about it at the time. It really was no big deal in those days. Looking back I could be a rich man now! I probably could have asked Jackson for "Black Betsy" and he would have given it to me!" Shoeless Joe Jackson died December 5, 1951 of a heart attack. Joe left everything to his wife Katie. Joe Anders was a pallbearer at the funeral held at Brandon Baptist Church in Greenville, SC. "There were so many flowers, you wouldn't have believed it. Even Charles Comiskey's grandson sent over a huge arrangement that looked like a miniature Comiskey Park," Anders said.

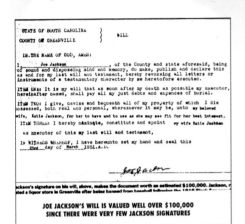

Today in Greenville, SC, the baseball field at Brandon Mill where Jackson started his career as a 13-year-old in 1901 has been renovated and renamed in his honor. Homeplate is now where center field used to be. The park was dedicated on March 30, 1996. Lights were added on March 30, 1999. 109 years after he was born, a section of highway was named for Joe. The "Shoeless Joe Jackson Museum" was opened on June 21, 2008 in West Greenville, SC and is the small red brick home he lived and died in.

Although Joe Anders passed away in 2015, it was his goal through his "Shoeless Joe Committee" that Jackson be reinstated back into baseball, then hopefully elected to the Hall of Fame. Anders felt as though it was the least he could do for his friend, and worked hard to bring attention to the cause. He traveled to Washington, DC to speak with politicians, and got Hall of Famers Ted Williams and Bob Feller to join the efforts. Their marquee names created more interest in the cause. Anders summarized the thoughts of many by saying "Shoeless served his sentence. It's time to put the man's name where it belongs: into the Hall of Fame in Cooperstown, NY."

The destination is chosen, the journey is in progress. While through a technicality, the first half

PHOTO BY DURHAM HUNT   SHOELESS JOE JACKSON'S GRAVE, WOODLAWN MEMORIAL PARK IN GREENVILLE, SC; DEBATED YEAR OF BIRTH IS OFF ONE YEAR

of Anders' wish was granted. In 2020, MLB admitted that once a player on the ineligible list passes away, his name is removed from the list and he is no longer banned from baseball. Now Joe's fate is in the hands of the Hall of Fame.

Movies such as "Field of Dreams," have rekindled interest in the event that rocked baseball some 100+ years ago. Ironically, the film was released in 1989 during baseball's most dismal season since 1919. Pete Rose was banned from baseball that same year. The storyline of "Field of Dreams" brings to light the true essence of the game that Shoeless Joe Jackson lived, loved and cherished all his days. It also draws parallels regarding missed chances and the desire for a second chance.

Shoeless Joe is a symbol of the triumphs and

PHOTO BY DURHAM HUNT   BALLFIELD WHERE JOE JACKSON LEARNED BASEBALL

tragedies of baseball. He was the All American boy who loved the game but got caught in the corruption of the people around him. He was trying to live life as a normal Joe and he carried his lost dreams with him to the grave, as so many do. In a way, the "Field of Dreams" movie site might be thought of as Shoeless Joe's personal Hall of Fame under the open blue skies of Dyersville, Iowa.

It is possible that the preservation and sharing of the "Field of Dreams" Movie Site is a better triumph of legacy and remembrance than a Hall of Fame induction. Enjoying the journey is what thousands of people young and old will cherish and remember for decades to come. Perhaps Joe did, after all, go the distance...

PHOTO BY DURHAM HUNT   HIGHWAY RENAMED IN 1996

By Nick Vetter, Low and Inside LLC

Special thanks to Joe Anders for the afternoon of stories and insight remembering the days with Shoeless Joe.

Thanks to Durham Hunt for the photography and insight on some historical scenery in Greenville, SC as it relates to Shoeless Joe.

Special thanks to Dan Wallach of the Shoeless Joe Jackson Museum and Library, for verifying information contained in this story. Visit ShoelessJoeJackson.org for more information on his legacy.

Last, but not least, "shoes off" to Joe Thompson. His 275+ page book titled, "Growing Up With Shoeless Joe" that will take you on a historical journey through Joe's life from his point of view.

1887   1951

He's been compared to the likes of Jimmy Stewart and Gary Cooper. He is able to play almost any part. From a hero to a romantic role. He's Kevin Costner and he's truly one of a kind.

PHOTO BY MELINDA SUE GORDON

Kevin was born in Lynwood, California, on January 18, 1955. He was the youngest of Bill Costner's two sons. His father, Bill, had a job that made them a bit nomadic. In fact during Kevin's high school days, he went to four different schools. This caused him to alter his personality many times to fit in, and at times forgot who he really was. Being of Irish, German, and Cherokee Indian descent also didn't help matters.

KEVIN BUILT A CANOE AND PADDLED DOWN THE SAME RIVERS AS LEWIS & CLARK DID.

During Kevin's school days, he did know that his primary interest was in sports. He played baseball, basketball, and football. He always dreamed of being a professional baseball player. Girls weren't a big part of his high school days. In fact he only had one date during this time! He was very shy and decided to find out who he really was for himself. At the age of 18, Kevin built a canoe and paddled his way down the same rivers as Lewis and Clark did on their way to the Pacific Ocean.

As for the family life while growing up, it was very normal. They were church goers and Kevin sang in the choir and also performed in the church musicals. He felt at this time acting was something he wanted to do but growing up in his family this seemed like something that could never be real.

Following high school, Kevin enlisted at California State in Fullerton. His first three years were uneventful as he majored in marketing. Then during his senior year life seemed to change one particular day as he read a class newspaper. Kevin saw an ad for auditions for "Rumplestiltskin." He didn't get a part, but his mind was ticking. He wanted to be an actor.

First, Costner found a community theater group. Here he learned the basics. It didn't get him very far, but the fire started burning. He soon graduated in 1978 with a degree in marketing and landed a job. After just six weeks he quit and dedicated everything to acting and his career on the screen. He then did a gutsy thing by moving to Hollywood with no agent or show biz connections. But, in his mind he was determined to succeed. Kevin wasn't planning on turning back or even on success or fame. He just knew it was in his heart. The move resulted in landing his first role in a movie called "Sizzle Beach." As a rookie, Kevin came out learning quite a bit about the industry.

At this time instead of following tradition and pounding doors for any bit-part or routine, he decided to start his own acting workshop. The workshop included writers and directors as well as other actors. They weren't making any money, but Kevin was happy because he was learning all the time.

Early in 1980, Costner went back into film acting and he has been with the industry ever since. He has always been very picky about the roles he portrays. Kevin has turned down many big box office roles such as the lead in "The Jagged Edge," or as Sargent Barnes in "Platoon." He also turned down parts in the movies "Big" and "Midnight Run" (the roles went to Tom Hanks and Robert DiNiro). Many people thought he was crazy for turning down some of those roles, but he just didn't feel comfortable with the scripts, and went with his gut feeling.

Then came along "Bull Durham." This part was just made for the sports enthusiast. Kevin played the character of Crash Davis flawlessly, but for him it wasn't a tough act to play since he always wanted to be a big leaguer. For him it was just playing himself. In fact, Costner ad-libbed many of the lines. The hard part about the movie "Bull Durham" was trying to get the finance and backing of a studio since shows about baseball met limited success at the box office.

Kevin took the role in another baseball movie and risked being labeled a "subject" actor. But when he read the script for "Field of Dreams" he knew he had to take the chance. The words seemed just so magical. He felt it would be a true mistake if he didn't play the role of Ray Kinsella. And the nice thing about it is it didn't categorize him as an actor like everyone said it would. It just helped make Kevin Costner that much better of a professional in his field.

By Rads E., Low and Inside LLC

Kevin Costner started a band "Modern West" whom have played live at "Field of Dreams." For more information visit KevinCostnerModernWest.com

COSTNER AT THE MOVIES

Malibu Hot Summer 1979	The Postman 1997
Chasing Dreams 1982	Message In A Bottle 1999
Night Shift 1982	For The Love Of The Game 1999
Frances 1982	Play It to the Bone 1999
Stacy's Nights 1983	Thirteen Days 2000
Table For Five 1983	3000 Miles to Graceland 2001
Testament 1983	Dragonfly 2002
The Gunrunner 1984	Open Range 2003
The Big Chill (role edited out)	The Upside of Anger 2005
Fandango 1985	Rumor Has It... 2005
Silverado 1985	The Guardian 2006
American Flyers 1985	Mr. Brooks 2007
Shadows Run Black 1986	Swing Vote 2008
Sizzle Beach U.S.A. 1986	The New Daughter 2009
The Untouchables 1987	The Company Men 2010
No Way Out 1987	Hatfields & McCoys 2012
Bull Durham 1988	Man of Steel 2013
Field of Dreams 1989	Jack Ryan: Shadow Recruit 2014
Revenge 1989	Draft Day 2014
Dances With Wolves 1990	Black or White 2014
Robin Hood Prince of Thieves 1991	3 Days to Kill 2014
J.F.K. 1991	McFarland 2015
Oliver Stone: Inside Out 1992	Criminal 2016
The Bodyguard 1992	Hidden Figures 2016
A Perfect World 1993	Molly's Game 2017
Wyatt Earp 1994	The Highwaymen 2019
The War 1994	Let Him Go 2020
Waterworld 1995	Yellowstone 2018-22
Tin Cup 1996	Horizon 2023

I'll bet the first time you saw the movie "Field of Dreams," you said to yourself, "Not too bad for a fictional show." But the more you looked into some of the players portrayed, the more real they seemed to be. That's because a few of them were.

IF YOU EVER GO TO THE TOWN OF CHISHOLM, MINNESOTA, YOU'LL FIND HE WAS AN EVEN BETTER HUMAN BEING THAN PORTRAYED IN THE MOVIE.

Now we all know "Shoeless Joe" Jackson, but I'd like to introduce you to Archibald (Doc) "Moonlight" Graham. To many of you this character probably seemed just too "Hollywood" too have ever existed. After all, nobody could have been that nice.

PHOTO BY LOW AND INSIDE

If you ever go to the town of Chisholm, Minnesota, you'll find he was an even better human being than portrayed in the movie.

"Moonlight" Graham did play in one major league game with the New York Giants. It was the last game of the season and the Giants had a 10-run lead. After eight innings, Manager John McGraw replaced George Browne in right field with "Moonlight" Graham. The game ended in less than five minutes with three infield outs. Graham then left baseball to pursue his dream to be a doctor.

A. W. "Moonlight" Graham
N. Y. Giants - Outfield

BASEBALL CARD SHOWN PRODUCED BY MIKE KALIBABKY IN SUPPORT OF THE "A.W. DOC GRAHAM MEMORIAL SCHOLARSHIP FUND"

THE GAME ENDED IN LESS THAN FIVE MINUTES WITH THREE INFIELD OUTS.

He settled in Chisholm, Minnesota one year after the 1908 Great Chisholm Fire. He spent six years

PHOTO BY LOW AND INSIDE

practicing at Chisholm's Rood Hospital before becoming physician for Chisholm Schools for the next 44 years. He was known in the community simply as "Doc" Graham.

"Field of Dreams" included several quirks or habits of "Doc's" that endeared him to the residents of Chisholm. He was a winker and he did always carry an umbrella on walks about town. His real life wife, Alecia, was fond of the color blue. Chisholm shop-keepers were happy to provide a variety of blue fabrics and accessories for him to choose from as he was a very generous man.

While he was the school doctor, his wife was a teacher. They were both active in the community. "Doc" is most remembered for his dedication to the

PHOTO BY LOW AND INSIDE   **VIEW OF DOWNTOWN CHISHOLM, MINNESOTA**

PHOTO BY LOW AND INSIDE   **A LOOK INSIDE THE NEWSPAPER OFFICE**

children. He was the team doctor who was considered part of the team and often thought oranges were the cure for everything. When he rode on the team bus, the kids knew they would all be fed. He always had loose change to share and would provide glasses to those in need. He also pioneered mandatory blood pressure screeening for children and is nationally recognized for his 13-year study on the effects of blood pressure on children.

GRAHAM ALSO PIONEERED MANDATORY BLOOD PRESSURE SCREEENING FOR CHILDREN

Alecia did not always completely approve of his carefree spending habits. On one occasion, he invited the basketball team and coaches for a special dinner at one of the hotels and picked up the whole tab because Alecia was out of town. He wanted to do something for the athletes as they were very special to him. In his opinion, everyone could be an athlete, even if for only half an inning.

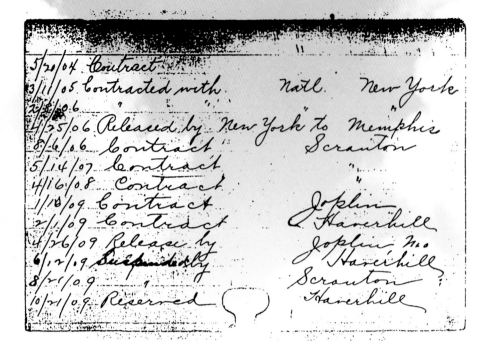

A.W. GRAHAM'S PROFESSIONAL BASEBALL CONTRACT CARD

There are other stories of children rubbing their eyes with onion in order to be sent to "Doc" Graham. With a diagnosis of pink eye and orders to go home, the children would head off to play ball. When "Doc" later discovered them at the ballpark, he merely joined the game and straightened out their improvised game of hooky.

THERE ARE OTHER STORIES OF CHILDREN RUBBING THEIR EYES WITH ONION IN ORDER TO BE SENT TO "DOC"

There were some "facts" in the "Field of Dreams" that were improvised to facilitate the story. He was not known in Chisholm as "Moonlight." Most folks were unaware he had ever played ball as he wasn't a reminiscent type of guy. Although the movie shows "Doc" walking down the street in 1972 (noted via a license plate), in reality, he passed away in 1965. He was survived by his wife Alecia, who passed away in 1981. The couple never did have children of their own but devoted their lives to the town's children.

Throughout his years in Chisholm, "Doc" Graham was considered a pillar of the community. Although there is nothing named after "Moonlight" Graham in Chisholm, a park located at the local school has been dedicated to the children. Called "Paradise City," it was renamed "Paradise City—A Field of Dreams" after the movie was released.

CHISHOLM, MINNESOTA NEWSPAPER OFFICE AS IT LOOKS IN PERSON

W.P. Kinsella, author of "Shoeless Joe," the book on which "Field of Dreams" is based, spent three days in Chisholm doing research for his book. He visited with Veda Ponikvar, who founded the "Chisholm Free Press" (local paper) and the person who actually wrote "Doc's" obituary.

Veda was a good friend of the Grahams. In fact, after "Doc" died, Mrs. Graham walked into the office wearing her usual blue, and handed Veda the only known photo of "Doc" when he was known as "Moonlight" Graham in the Giants uniform. Alecia said, "I don't know of anyone who would appreciate this more than you, Veda." She worked on projects with the Graham's and became close through the years.

Kinsella first became intrigued by a name in "The Baseball Encyclopedia" along with its unusual stats. He had hoped for a person with a history of alcoholism, drug abuse, child neglect or midnight abortions to cloud his past. Much to his surprise, he found a man whose generosity and goodness is still remembered today. A man almost too good to be true by Hollywood standards.

May the light of "Moonlight" Graham shine on in the darkness of the world today.

By Nick Vetter, Low and Inside LLC

PHOTO BY LOW AND INSIDE

DOC GRAHAM'S HOUSE; TODAY IT IS AN APARTMENT BUILDING

A special thanks to the city of Chisholm, Minnesota, and in particular, Mike Kalibabky and Veda Ponikvar for their time and historical insight.

"Doc Moonlight Graham Days" are held in the city of Chisholm MN each year during the first weekend of August. Visit the Chisholm Area Chamber of Commerce online for more information.

PHOTO BY LOW AND INSIDE

"PARADISE CITY – A FIELD OF DREAMS" LOCATED IN CHISHOLM, MINNESOTA ON A COMMUNITY SCHOOLYARD

■ MILT GRAFF	Graff, Milton Edward	b: 12/30/30, Jefferson Center, Pa.	BL/TR, 5'7.5", 158 lbs.	Deb: 4/16/57	C																				
1957	KC-A	56	155	16	28	4	3	0	10	15	10	.181	.262	.245	.507	40	-13	-13	99	104	10	.429	2	5	-2	-7
1958	KC-A	5	1	0	0	0	0	0	0	0	0	.000	.000	.000	.000	-95	-0	-0	106	0	0	.000	0	0	0	0
Total 2		61	156	16	28	4	3	0	10	15	10	.179	.260	.244	.504	39	-13	-13	99	103	10	.429	2	5	-2	-7
■ MOONLIGHT GRAHAM	Graham, Archibald Wright	b: 11/9/1876, Fayetteville, N.C.	d: 8/25/65, Chisolm, Minn.	5'10.5", 170 lbs.	Deb: 6/29/05																				
1905	NY-N	1	0	0	0	0	0	0	0	0	—	—	—	—	0	0	101	—	—	—	0		0		
■ SKINNY GRAHAM	Graham, Arthur William	b: 8/12/09, Somerville, Mass.	d: 7/10/67, Cambridge, Mass.	BL/TR, 5'7", 162 lbs.	Deb: 9/14/34																				
1934	Bos-A	13	47	7	11	2	1	0	3	6	13	.234	.321	.319	.640	62	-2	-3	106	68	5	.605	2	2	-1	-1
1935	Bos-A	8	10	1	3	0	0	0	1	1	3	.300	.364	.300	.664	68	-0	-0	108	113	1	.714	1	0	0	-1
Total 2		21	57	8	14	2	1	0	4	7	16	.246	.328	.316	.644	63	-3	-3	106	76	6	.622	3	2	-0	-2

MOONLIGHT GRAHAM'S LISTING FROM THE BASEBALL ENCYCLOPEDIA

ARCHIBALD MOONLIGHT GRAHAM

A name forgotten until Hollywood,
But always curious to the stat fan.
A story of unforgotten memories,
At 0-0 his numbers did stand.
He had lived in Chisholm, Minnesota,
that's where his true heart did lie.
But he would often talk about that special day,
Until the time he did die.
With the Charlotte Hornets—North Carolina League,
that's where his minor league days were at.
And after the call from the NY Giants,
He thought it was his time to swing a major league bat.
It was on June 29, 1905,
He thought that dream was near.
Everything seemed perfect,
Everything seemed so clear.
With a 10-run lead over the Dodgers,
8 innings into the game.
Manager John McGraw,
Screamed out his name.
George Browne was the man called in,
To the field Moonlight took.
5 minutes later—three infield outs,
Moonlight never took another look.
Retirement—back to school,
That's were he did go.
Always wondering was I good enough,
He never would know.
Doc pursued the dream of medicine,
and dedicated his life to kids.
The town of Chisholm remembers him,
For all the good works he did.
Everything worked out just fine,
His dreams did bring him some fame.
A legacy is your story,
And people knowing your name.

By Scott Mahlmann, Low and Inside LLC

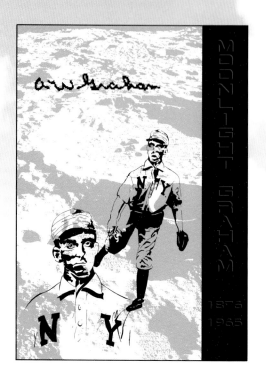

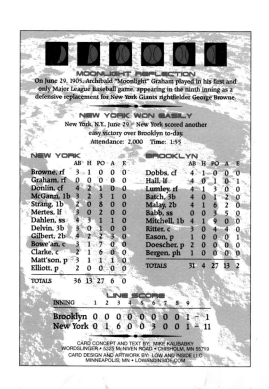

MOONLIGHT REFLECTION
On June 29, 1905, Archibald "Moonlight" Graham played in his first and only Major League Baseball game, appearing in the ninth inning as a defensive replacement for New York Giants rightfielder George Browne.

NEW YORK WON EASILY
New York, N.Y., June 29 – New York scored another easy victory over Brooklyn to-day.
Attendance: 2,000 Time: 1:55

NEW YORK	AB	H	PO	A	E
Browne, rf	3	1	0	0	0
Graham, rf	0	0	0	0	0
Donlin, cf	4	2	1	0	0
McGann, 1b	3	2	3	1	0
Strang, 1b	2	0	8	0	0
Mertes, lf	3	0	2	0	0
Dahlen, ss	4	3	1	1	0
Delvin, 3b	3	0	1	0	0
Gilbert, 2b	4	2	2	3	0
Bowe'an, c	3	1	7	0	0
Clarke, c	2	1	6	0	0
Matt'son, p	3	1	1	1	0
Elliott, p	2	0	0	0	0
TOTALS	36	13	27	6	0

BROOKLYN	AB	H	PO	A	E
Dobbs, cf	4	1	0	0	0
Hall, lf	4	0	1	0	1
Lumley, rf	4	1	3	0	0
Batch, 3b	4	0	1	2	0
Malay, 2b	4	1	6	2	0
Babb, ss	0	0	3	5	0
Mitchell, 1b	4	1	9	0	0
Ritter, c	3	0	4	4	0
Eason, p	1	0	0	0	1
Doescher, p	2	0	0	0	0
Bergen, ph	1	0	0	0	0
TOTALS	31	4	27	13	2

LINE SCORE

INNING	1	2	3	4	5	6	7	8	9		
Brooklyn	0	0	0	0	0	0	0	1	0	–	1
New York	0	1	6	0	0	3	0	0	1	–	11

CARD CONCEPT AND TEXT BY: MIKE KALIBABKY
WORDSLINGER • 5325 McNIVEN ROAD • CHISHOLM, MN 55719
CARD DESIGN AND ARTWORK BY: LOW AND INSIDE LLC
MINNEAPOLIS, MN • LOWANDINSIDE.COM

- ❑ **Dreams**
- ❑ **Corn**
- ❑ **Iowa**
- ❑ **Movie**
- ❑ **Field**
- ❑ **Plow**
- ❑ **Fatherhood**
- ❑ **Memories**
- ❑ **Swing**
- ❑ **Catch**
- ❑ Kevin **Costner**
- ❑ **Shoeless** Joe Jackson
- ❑ Don **Lansing**
- ❑ W.P. **Kinsella**
- ❑ Doc **Graham**
- ❑ **Heaven**
- ❑ Rita & Al **Ameskamp**
- ❑ **Dyersville**
- ❑ **Porch**
- ❑ **Amy** Madigan

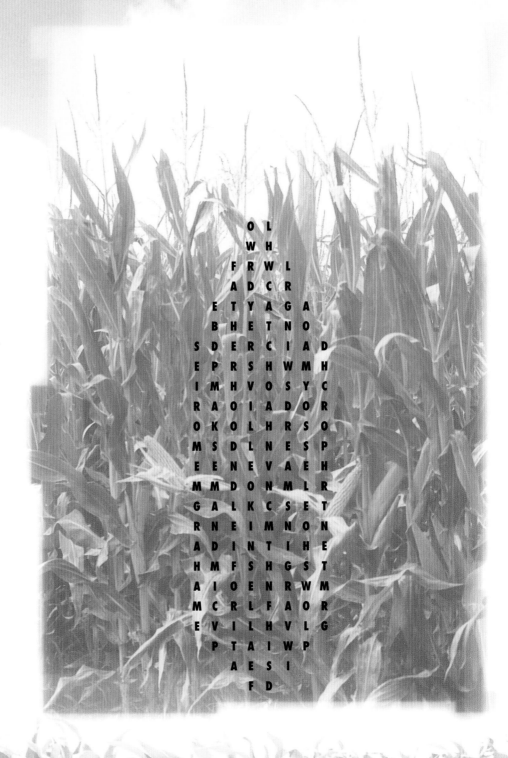

```
          O  L
          W  H
    F  R  W  L
    A  D  C  R
    E  T  Y  A  G  A
    B  H  E  T  N  O
  S D  E  R  C  I  A  D
  E P  R  S  H  W  M  H
  I M  H  V  O  S  Y  C
  R A  O  I  A  D  O  R
  O K  O  L  H  R  S  O
  M S  D  L  N  E  S  P
  E E  N  E  V  A  E  H
  M M  D  O  N  M  L  R
  G A  L  K  C  S  E  T
  R N  E  I  M  N  O  N
  A D  I  N  T  I  H  E
  H M  F  S  H  G  S  T
  A I  O  E  N  R  W  M
  M C  R  L  F  A  O  R
  E V  I  L  H  V  L  G
  P T  A  I  W  P
  A E  S  I
  F D
```

Find the words (bold-faced) in the puzzle and take a trip back to the last time you went to or saw the Field of Dreams.

JOE LEGACY
SHOELESS JOE MUSEUM

The Shoeless Joe Jackson Museum and Baseball Library is located in Greenville, South Carolina, just across the street from Fluor Field in Greenville's historic West End. The Greenville Drive, a High-A affiliate of the Boston Red Sox, play their home games at the mini-Fenway Park, fully-equipped with a Green Monster in left field.

FLUOR FIELD ENTRANCE - SHOELESS JOE JACKSON STATUE   PHOTO BY LOW AND INSIDE

The museum is housed inside Joe and Katie Jackson's former home, which was moved from its original location in 2006 and renovated to become the museum. An addition built in 2021 doubled their size and allowed the SJJM to expand the gift shop, adding some interactive displays and photo ops, while allowing the entirety of the house to function as the museum.

SHOELESS JOE JACKSON MUSEUM & BASEBALL LIBRARY   PHOTO BY LOW AND INSIDE

VISITORS OF THE MUSEUM WILL LEARN HOW JACKSON GOT HIS START PLAYING BASEBALL

Visitors of the museum will learn how Jackson got his start playing baseball in Greenville's Textile League, which eventually led to Joe being discovered by a local semi-pro team, the Greenville Spinners. You will learn the true story of how Joe got his nickname in 1908 while playing for the Spinners before getting called up to the Major Leagues. The museum tells the story of Joe's burgeoning baseball career before his time with the White Sox, when he played in Philadelphia, Savannah, New Orleans, and Cleveland while bouncing back and forth between the Majors and Minor Leagues.

An entire room of the museum is dedicated to Joe's time with Chicago, and you will learn the truth behind the Black Sox Scandal of the 1919 World Series, backed by the latest research uncovered and published by the Society for American Baseball Research (SABR). You will un-learn everything you thought you knew about the scandal, as the museum does a great job of presenting information to debunk century-old myths and

JOE JACKSON MUSEUM HISTORICAL ITEMS & PHOTOS   PHOTO BY LOW AND INSIDE

providing the proper context for what really happened, and why. Nearly all visitors of the museum come in asking "Did Joe really throw the World Series?" By the time they leave, they'll have the answer.

THE MUSEUM HAS A LARGE BASEBALL LIBRARY WITH MANY UNIQUE BOOKS

Where the museum truly excels is telling the story of Joe's life and continued baseball career after his banishment from MLB. See pictures of Joe during

SHOELESS JOE JACKSON FRONT DOOR AT .356 FIELD ST.   PHOTO BY LOW AND INSIDE

his barnstorming years in Georgia, and his return back home to South Carolina to play Textile League ball. Learn about the businesses he and his wife, Katie, ran throughout life, appreciating how instrumental she was to their financial success.

SHOELESS JOE JACKSON MUSEUM WHITE SOX ROOM   PHOTO BY LOW AND INSIDE

Joe Jackson started working in the cotton mills at the age of 6 and never went to school a day in his life. Consequently, he never had the chance to learn how to read or write. You'll learn how, despite that, many fans over the years received a signature which said "Joe Jackson," and you'll even see one for yourself. You'll also hear about Joe Jackson's Liquor Store, and can touch the doorknob on the original doors from that business — the same one Ty Cobb touched when he visited Joe in 1947.

GRAB A JOE JACKSON REPLICA BAT FOR YOUR PHOTO OP   PHOTO BY LOW AND INSIDE

As long as you're in Greenville, there are lots of other Joe Jackson-related sites to see: the site of the liquor store, Brandon Mill and the Brandon Mill ball field (which has since been renamed "Shoeless Joe Jackson Memorial Park") where Joe got his start playing ball as a 13-year-old, and Joe and Katie's gravesite, to name a few.

SHOELESS JOE JACKSON'S ORIGINAL OFFICE AND PHONE   PHOTO BY LOW AND INSIDE

PLAQUE AT FLUOR FIELD PHOTO BY LOW AND INSIDE

SHOELESS JOE JACKSON MUSEUM & BASEBALL LIBRARY HISTORICAL PLAQUE IN FRONT PHOTO BY LOW AND INSIDE

In an effort to document and preserve some of Jackson's history, the SJJM has launched a community book box project, making free books available to the local communities in which the boxes are placed. Since Joe was famously illiterate, one of the museum's missions is to promote literacy in his name. These boxes will be placed in locations which are relevant to Joe's life and career, in Greenville and across the country. You can learn more about the program on the museum's website, where you can also donate to help support the cause.

VISIT BEAUTIFUL GREENVILLE, SC AND DISCOVER THE HISTORICAL MAGIC OF THE CITY

There are lots of wonderful places to visit and explore in Greenville that aren't baseball-related, as well, and it's a great little city to spend a long weekend. In the meantime, become a member of the museum by visiting their website ShoelessJoeJackson.org and follow them on social media @ShoelessMuseum.

By Dan Wallach, Former Executive Director of the Shoeless Joe Jackson Museum and Library in Greenville SC who is passionate about baseball and the preservation of it's storied history.

PLAQUE LOCATED AT FLUOR FIELD ACROSS FROM MUSEUM PHOTO BY LOW AND INSIDE

JOE JACKSON'S LIQUOR STORE LOCATION PHOTO BY LOW AND INSIDE

THE GIFT SHOP IS VERY EXTENSIVE AT THE MUSEUM PHOTO BY LOW AND INSIDE

LORI AND DAN WALLACH - FORMER MUSEUM EXECUTIVE DIRECTOR PHOTO BY LOW AND INSIDE

SHOELESS JOE JACKSON MEMORIAL PARK PHOTO BY LOW AND INSIDE

SHOELESS JOE JACKSON MUSEUM AND BASEBALL LIBARARY
356 Field Street • Greenville SC 29601
ShoelessJoeJackson.org

MEDITATION
PERSONAL REFLECTION

PHOTO BY LOW AND INSIDE

EXPERIENCE THE MAGIC...

MOVIE TRIVIA
A SCREEN TEST

1. What name was on Terence Mann's mailbox?
2. Who did Burt Lancaster play in the movie?
3. What year did Shoeless Joe Jackson die?
4. For what team did Doc Graham play?
5. Of what national ancestry was Ray Kinsella?

19. When Terence and Ray were on the road driving, what was sitting on the dashboard?
20. What was Alecia Graham's favorite color?
21. What position did Ray Kinsella's dad play in the minor leagues?

PHOTO BY PHOTO BY LOW AND INSIDE

ANSWERS:

1. Tye Dyed 2. Moonlight Graham 3. 1951
4. New York Giants 5. Irish 6. Karen 7. "The Godfather"
8. Freedom of Speech (no book burning) 9. John
10. Terence Mann 11. 1952 12. Seat #1
13. Moonlight Graham 14. Rosebud
15. Himself (the secret is still kept) 16. First base side, about halfway up 17. "The Boatrocker" by Terence Mann 18. 1972
19. A book, "The Baseball Encyclopedia" 20. Blue 21. Catcher
22. A piece of hot dog 23. Ray Liotta 24. Phil Alden Robinson
25. Volkswagen

DREAM-O-METER:

5 OR LESS RIGHT
Think you better restart the movie and press "play" again.

ABOUT HALF RIGHT
Pause on the DVD player must have failed after 1/2 hour, huh?!

5 OR LESS WRONG
Can see you have watched this more than three times.

ALL 25 RIGHT
You are an "Academy Award" winner!

PHOTO BY STEPHEN GASSMAN

6. What was Annie and Ray's daughter's name?
7. At the Plaza Theater in Chisholm, MN, what film was playing when Ray "went back in time?"
8. In the movie, what Constitutional Right did Annie stand up for?
9. What was the name of Ray Kinsella's dad?
10. Who did Ray kidnap in Boston, MA?
11. Kevin Costner played Ray Kinsella. In what year was Ray born?
12. What was the seat number Ray sat in at Fenway Park?
13. Who did Terence and Ray want to find in Chisholm, MN?
14. Annie jokingly refers to Terence Mann once having a bat he nicknamed what?
15. Who in the credits is "The Voice?"
16. On what side of the diamond was Ray sitting in Fenway Park?
17. At age 17, what book did Ray read that caused him to break away from his father?
18. What year did Ray uncover on the license plate in Chisholm when he "fell back in time?"

22. What did Karin choke on after she fell?
23. Who played Shoeless Joe in the movie?
24. Who directed the film?
25. What make of van did Ray Kinsella have?

PHOTO BY LOW AND INSIDE

FIELD OF DREAMS MOVIE SITE VIEWED FROM LANSING ROAD

PHOTO BY AMERICAN IMAGES

The Academy Award nominee for "Best Picture of the Year" in 1989, "Field of Dreams," has affected the public in a way seldom matched in movie history. With its themes of family ties, faith, second chances and the special relationship between baseball and the American people, the movie has, in just few short years, woven itself permanently into the fabric of life in the United States.

PHOTO BY LOW AND INSIDE

What is especially gratifying today, is that so much of the magic still remains. The green grass, the dirt infield, the unforgettable farmhouse with its cozy porch swing and picket fence and even the bleachers with a carved heart that proclaims "Ray Loves Annie."

Visiting the Field of Dreams Movie Site is worth putting on your family's list of destinations. It will have a different effect on every person who takes the time to stop by and reflect on what "going the distance" has personally meant to them.

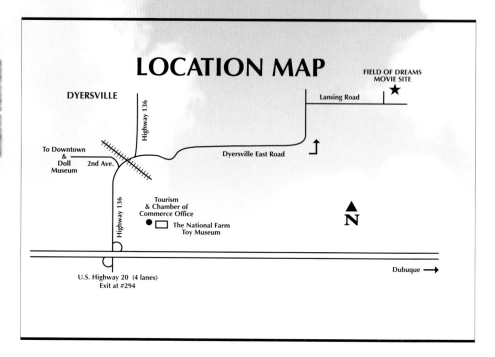

LOCATION MAP

FIELD OF DREAMS MOVIE SITE ★

DYERSVILLE

Highway 136

Lansing Road

To Downtown & Doll Museum

2nd Ave.

Dyersville East Road

Highway 136

Tourism & Chamber of Commerce Office

The National Farm Toy Museum

▲ N

U.S. Highway 20 (4 lanes) Exit at #294

Dubuque →

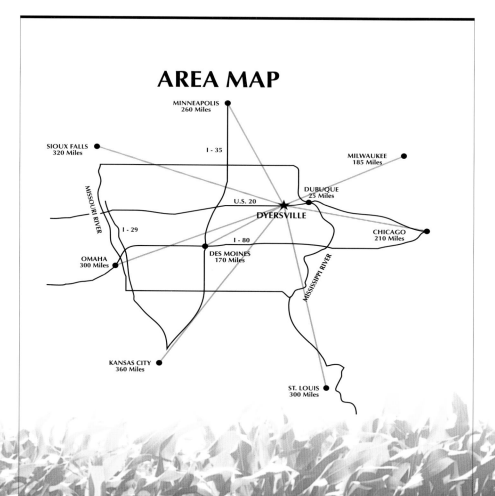

AREA MAP

MINNEAPOLIS 260 Miles

SIOUX FALLS 320 Miles

I - 35

MILWAUKEE 185 Miles

MISSOURI RIVER

DUBUQUE 25 Miles

U.S. 20

DYERSVILLE

I - 29

I - 80

CHICAGO 210 Miles

OMAHA 300 Miles

DES MOINES 170 Miles

MISSISSIPPI RIVER

KANSAS CITY 360 Miles

ST. LOUIS 300 Miles

25 MOST ASKED QUESTIONS

1. Who owns the Field of Dreams?
An Iowa-based investment group, Go The Distance Baseball, LLC currently owns the "Field of Dreams." The majority of the Field of Dreams Movie Site including the house, the infield, right field and part of center field were originally owned by Becky and Don Lansing. Left field and part of center field were owned by Rita & Al Ameskamp until 2010.

2. Does anyone live in the house at the Field of Dreams?
Yes. One of the owners of Go The Distance Baseball, LLC, lives on-site now to help maintain the property that also is used as event and office space.

3. Out of all the farms, why here?
It met all Hollywood's criteria and typified the traditional all-American farm. This farm looked like the one-man operation and had rolling hills for easier lighting while shooting. The sunset direction was also a factor among other things.

4. Who takes care of the Field?
Original owner Don Lansing still helps care for the Field with other staff and contractors.

5. When did the first visitor stop by the Field of Dreams?
On May 5, 1989, a guy from New York stopped by on his way to California.

6. About how many show up on the average weekend?
There is a steady flow of people all the time. During peak weekends, over 3,000 is common.

7. What's the furthest distance someone has come to visit?
People from Japan and Australia have come as well as those from other European countries.

8. Is the same swing used in the movie still on the porch?
No. One was rented from a house in Dubuque. One that closely resembles that one was installed after shooting.

9. Do the lights still work?
Yes they still work.

10. Were there changes made to the house?
Yes. The porch was extended and a couple large bay windows were added. A few evergreen trees were removed as well as other cosmetic updates.

11. How long did it take to build the Field?
Hollywood built it in just 4 days during the summer of 1988.

12. How long was the actual movie shooting on location?
Shooting live action lasted for 9 weeks during the hot summer of 1988.

13. Where did the actors stay while shooting at the Field?
Most of the actors stayed in Dubuque & Galena, IL as well as other places around the countryside.

14. Are there special events staged at Field of Dreams?
Efforts are taken not to over commercialize the movie site, but there have been a few events staged at the Field in the past. Also, The Ghost Players team appear from out of the corn throughout the summer.

15. When can I visit the Field of Dreams Movie Site?
Hours for visiting from April through October are, 9:00 a.m. to 6:00 p.m. and weekends only in November. Please visit the calendar of events on our website fodmoviesite.com for current hours of operation.

16. Have any famous people stopped in to see the place?
Everyone is special who visits. But some of those recognizable names have been Reggie Jackson, Ernie Banks, Bob Feller, Sadaharu Oh, Bob Gibson, Kirby Puckett, & Lou Brock.

17. Has actor Kevin Costner come back to visit the Field yet?
Yes he and his band Modern West, have returned to the "Field of Dreams" in the past.

18. Did the Hollywood people treat the local folks well, and did they like Iowa?
From all reports, the cast and crew were exceptionally easy to have here. Many who spoke with—even got to know—Kevin Costner speak highly of him and his down-to-earth style. The producer of the film, Brian Frankish, still keeps in touch with some of his Dyersville friends. Many of the cast and crew admitted to being amazed at the beautiful countryside of this area. They remarked on the friendliness of the people, the cleanliness, and the quiet atmosphere. One of the sound men "complained" that it was almost too quiet for his equipment, which was programmed to eliminate the usual outside noise. He was glad, however, that his equipment could do its job the night when his headset was filled with the summer-evening sound of crickets!

19. Who were other celebs, besides Costner, who starred in the movie?
James Earl Jones (Terence Mann), Amy Madigan (Annie Kinsella), Burt Lancaster ("Doc" Graham), Ray Liotta (Shoeless Joe), and Timothy Busfield (Mark), Dwier Brown (John Kinsella).

20. Is there any charge for visiting the Field of Dreams Movie Site?
No, admission is not charged to visit the Field. There are however, donation boxes and proceeds are used to offset maintenance costs.

21. Who carved the "Ray Loves Annie" in a heart on the top row of the Field's bleachers?
Kevin Costner himself, while bored between movie takes at the Field of Dreams.

22. Did Field of Dreams win any awards?
It was nominated for the following in 1989:

Nominee: Best Picture of the Year
Charles Gordon - Producer

Nominee: Best Picture of the Year
Lawrence Gordon - Producer

Nominee: Best Screenplay Based on Material From Another Medium - Phil Alden Robinson

Nominee: Best Achievement in Music (Original Score)
James Horner

23. How did they get all the cars to drive in for the last scene?
The film's publicist ran an advertisement with an entry form in the local newspaper. Anyone interested in participating in the final scene could send in the form. The first 1,500 entries were sent a pass, enabling them and a passenger to ride in their vehicle. There were three takes—the third one was used in the movie, with the drivers rapidly changing their lights from bright to dim, to give the twinkling effect. This scene was shot from a helicopter.

24. Who drove in the first car to the Field for the final scene?
Don Lansing drove the first car in line to the Field of Dreams along with Phil Alden Robinson.

25. How long will the site's owners continue to keep the Field of Dreams going?
They have said they will keep the Field open as long as there are people coming to see it.

FUN AND GAMES
FOR THE ROAD TRIP HOME

IOWA SITES & SCENERY
HOW MANY LETTERS OF THE ALPHABET CAN YOU FILL IN?
(EXAMPLE: C = CORN)

A _____
B _____
C _____
D _____
E _____
F _____
G _____
H _____
I _____
J _____
K _____
L _____
M _____
N _____
O _____
P _____
Q _____
R _____
S _____
T _____
U _____
V _____
W _____
X _____
Y _____
Z _____

LIST BALLPARKS YOU SEE ON YOUR WAY...

CONNECT THE DOTS